The Sermon on the Mount

The Sermon on the Mount
D. A. Carson

AN EVANGELICAL OF MATTHEW 5-7 EXPOSITION

BAKER BOOK HOUSE
Grand Rapids, Michigan 49516

TO CICCU

in grateful appreciation
for the warmth of your Christian witness
and for the opportunity to teach you
such a challenging part
of the Scriptures

CONTENTS

PREFACE

Early in 1974 I was asked to give six addresses on the Sermon on the Mount to the Cambridge Inter-Collegiate Christian Union (CICCU). These addresses, slated for the Easter term of 1975, consumed a large part of my time and energy for the six weeks over which they were spread. I do not think I have ever enjoyed teaching people the Scriptures as much as I enjoyed speaking to the four or five hundred students who gathered every Saturday night. Unusually receptive, they challenged me by their genuine attentiveness to the Word of God.

Since then I have repeated the series two or three times, in churches located in British Columbia. As time has permitted, I have revised the series, writing it in a form more congenial to the printed page than a sermon or Bible reading usually is. However, I have deliberately not removed all traces of the earlier form. I have added two appendices, largely elicited by questions that have been put to me. Some of the material in the first appendix was interwoven into the original series, but I have thought it best in this book to separate it.

How does this volume differ from those now in circulation which deal with the same passage? Why offer another study on the Sermon on the Mount? Several reasons spring to mind. This exposition is shorter than most others designed for the general reader; but that is because it is more condensed. I have tried hard to be freer from the categories of systematic theology than some of my predecessors, though I want my work to be informed by the most significant theological points of view. The material in the two appendices is not usually included in popular expositions, but it may help the interested reader to view the interpretation of the Sermon on the Mount with a more balanced vision and with deeper understanding. But more than any other reason, I am offering these studies to a larger circle because I am deeply convinced that the church of Christ needs to study the Sermon on the Mount again and again.

I take pleasure in recording here my deep gratitude to many scores of writers. I have read some of the popular expositions, but apart from the sacred text itself I have made it a point above all to read the best commentaries I could secure. W. S. Kissinger's *The Sermon on the Mount: A History of Interpretation and Bibliography* has been an invaluable tool in the later stages of study. A gold mine of information, it introduced me to some serious works of which I was quite unaware. Informed readers will also sense my indebtedness to Robert Banks' *Jesus and the Law in the Synoptic Tradition.* I want to record my thanks to Tyndale House, Cambridge, which afforded me the opportunity to read a copy of Banks' doctoral dissertation before his published revision put in an appearance. I have read only a few foreign language works on the Sermon on the Mount. This I regret, just as I regret that I could not canvass more of the enormous body of secondary literature. Even in the journals that have crossed my desk during the past quarter there has not been any shortage of studies on these three chapters of Matthew's Gospel.

My sincere gratitude is also extended to Eileen Appleby, who transcribed the tapes of the original addresses; and to Sue Wonnacott, and especially to Diane Smith, who transformed an excessively messy manuscript into neat and near-flawless typescript.

Soli Deo Gloria.

D. A. Carson
Northwest Baptist Theological Seminary
Vancouver, Canada

1 MATTHEW 5:1-16

THE KINGDOM OF HEAVEN:
Its Norms and Witness

INTRODUCTION

The more I read these three chapters—Matthew 5, 6 and 7—the more I am both drawn to them and shamed by them. Their brilliant light draws me like a moth to a spotlight; but the light is so bright that it sears and burns. No room is left for forms of piety which are nothing more than veneer and sham. Perfection is demanded. Jesus says, "Be perfect . . . as your heavenly Father is perfect" (5:48).

The great theme of these three chapters is the kingdom of heaven. "The kingdom of heaven" is Matthew's customary expression for what other New Testament writers preferred to call "the kingdom of God." Matthew was like many Jews of his day who would avoid using the word "God." They felt it was too holy, too exalted; therefore euphemisms like "heaven" were adopted. In meaning, kingdom of heaven is identical to kingdom of God (cf. Matt. 19:23f.; Mark 10:23f.; etc.).

Four preliminary observations may help to clarify these expressions. First, the idea of "kingdom" in both the Old and New Testaments is primarily dynamic rather than spatial. It is not so much a kingdom with geographical borders as it is a "kingdominion," or reign. In the Scriptures, the spatial meaning of kingdom is secondary and derivative.

Second, although the kingdom of God can refer to the totality of God's sovereignty, that is not what is in view in the Sermon on the Mount. Indeed, in the universal sense, God's kingdom—his reign—is eternal and all-embracing. No one and nothing can escape from it. From the time of Jesus' resurrection and exaltation onward, all of this divine sovereignty is mediated through Christ. Jesus himself taught this: "All authority in heaven and on earth has been given to me" (Matt. 28:18). This universal authority is what Paul refers to when he says that Christ must reign until God has put all his enemies under his feet (I Cor. 15:25). Some refer to this "kingdom" as the mediatorial kingdom of God, because God's authority, his reign, is mediated through Christ.

But this cannot be the kingdom of God most frequently in view in the New Testament. In the Sermon on the Mount, not everyone enters the kingdom of heaven, but only those who are poor in spirit (5:3), obedient (7:21), and surpassingly righteous (5:20). Similarly, in John's Gospel, only he who is born from above can see or enter the kingdom of God (John 3:3, 5). Since the universal kingdom by definition must include everyone whether he likes it or not, we see that the kingdom in these passages cannot be universal. There are conditions to be met before entrance is possible. The kingdom with which I am concerned in these essays, the kingdom preached by Jesus, is a *subset* of the universal kingdom.

We get an idea what is meant when we compare Mark 9:45 and Mark 9:47. The first verse reads: "And if your foot causes you to sin, cut it off. It is better for you to *enter life* crippled, than to have two feet and be thrown into hell." The second reads: "And if your eye causes you to sin, pluck it out. It is better for you to *enter the kingdom of God* with one eye, than to have two eyes and be thrown into hell." To enter the kingdom of God, then, is to enter life. That is characteristically the language of John's Gospel; however, it is found in the Sermon on the Mount itself. These three chapters of Matthew are concerned with entering the kingdom (Matt. 5:3, 10; 7:21), which is equivalent to entering into life (7:13f.; cf. 19:14, 16).

Thus the kingdom of heaven in this narrower sense is that exercise of God's sovereignty which bears directly on his saving purposes. All who are in the kingdom have life; all who are not in the kingdom do not have life. We might schematize these conclusions as follows:

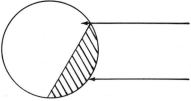

The universal kingdom of God, now mediated through Christ

The kingdom of God: that aspect of the universal kingdom under which there is life

Or, if God's saving purposes lie at the heart of his sovereignty, the scheme might be improved thus:

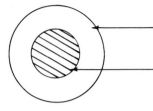

The universal kingdom of God, now mediated through Christ

The kingdom of God: that aspect of the universal kingdom under which there is life

Of course, this diagram over-schematizes the evidence. The word "kingdom," having primary reference to the dynamic, can be used in the more extended sense or the special salvific sense. For example, Jesus elsewhere tells a parable in which he likens the kingdom to a man who sowed good seed in his field, yet discovered weeds sprouting up, sown by an enemy (Matt. 13:24-29, 36-43). It appears as if the kingdom at this point embraces both wheat and weeds; in non-metaphorical terms, the kingdom embraces both men with life and men without life. In terms of the circular diagram above, the line between the inner circle and the outer becomes very thin. The emphasis seems to be on the universal kingdom, even though the sowing of good seed is its central purpose. Indeed, as a result of that purpose, the present mixed crop one day gets sorted out: at harvest time, the weeds are tied into bundles and burned, and the wheat is gathered into the master's barn (Matt. 13:30).

This ambiguity helps us to understand Matthew 8:10-12, where Jesus says, "I tell you the truth, I have not found anyone in Israel with such great faith. I say to you that many will come from the east and the west, and will take their places at the feast with Abraham, Isaac and Jacob in the kingdom of heaven. But the subjects of the kingdom will be thrown outside, into the darkness, where there will be weeping and grinding of teeth." The Jews, privileged as they were to be the inheritors of the Old Testament revelation, were the expected "subjects of the kingdom"; but Jesus indicates that in fact many from all over the world will join the patriarchs in the kingdom. He also warns that many expected subjects will be excluded from the delights of God's saving reign.

Third, the expression "kingdom of God," in the saving sense (the only way I will use it from now on), applies to both present and future. Taken together, the books of the New Testament insist that the kingdom of God has already arrived; a person may enter the kingdom and receive life now, life "to the full" (John 10:10). Jesus himself argues that if he drives out demons by the Spirit of God—and he does—then the kingdom of God *has come* (Matt. 12:28). Nevertheless, the books of the New Testament insist that the kingdom will be inherited only in the future, when Christ comes again. Eternal life, though experienced now, is con-summated then, in conjunction with such a renovation of the universe that the only adequate description is "a new heaven and a new earth" (Isa. 65:17; 66:22; II Peter 3:13; Rev. 21:1; cf. Rom. 8:21ff.).

Jesus tells several parables with the specific purpose of removing mis-conceptions among his followers, misconceptions to the effect that the full arrival of the kingdom would be achieved without any delay. He wanted them to think otherwise: the coming of the kingdom in its fulness might well require significant delay. For example, in one parable in Luke's Gospel (Luke 19:11ff.), Jesus pictures a man of noble birth who goes to a distant country and then returns; and he receives full au-thority of a kingdom only after he has returned. Jesus is that nobleman, and the consummation of the kingdom awaits his return.

Another diagram might help to explain these truths:

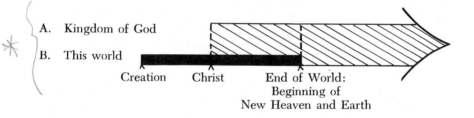

A.   Kingdom of God

B.   This world

Creation   Christ   End of World:
Beginning of
New Heaven and Earth

All men live on the plane of "this world"; but from the time of Christ's coming to the end of the world, the inheritors of the kingdom (and they alone) also live on the plane of the kingdom. Thus, from the circular diagrams it is clear that a man may or may not be in the kingdom of God; from the linear sketch it is clear that if he is in it now, he may yet look forward to its consummation at the end of the world, when Christ re-turns. There is an "already" aspect of the kingdom, and a "not yet" as-pect: the kingdom has already come, but it has not yet arrived.

Fourth, although entering into life and entering the kingdom are synonymous, they are not always strictly interchangeable. The very idea of "kingdom" as "dynamic reign" brings with it overtones of authority and submission not normally conjured up when we speak of "life." The kingdom of God speaks of God's authority, mediated through Christ; therefore it speaks equally of our whole-hearted allegiance to that authority. That is why Matthew 7:21-23 so stresses obedience: "Not everyone who says to me, 'Lord, Lord,' will enter the kingdom of heaven, but only he who does the will of my Father who is in heaven. Many will say to me in that day, 'Lord, Lord, did we not prophesy in your name, and in your name drive out demons and perform many miracles?' Then I will tell them plainly, 'I never knew you. Away from me, you evil-doers!' "

It is the kingdom of heaven, then, that is the great theme of the Sermon on the Mount. At the end of Matthew 4 we learn that Jesus went throughout Galilee "preaching the good news of the kingdom" (4:23). Both his preaching and his miracles of healing attracted large crowds to him. Accordingly Matthew 5 opens with the words, "Now when he saw the crowds, he went up on a mountainside and sat down. His disciples came to him, and he began to teach them." Some have urged that Jesus' response to the crowds was to withdraw and train his disciples. By training them Jesus would be multiplying his own ministry. This probably reads too much into the text, for in Matthew's Gospel "disciple" is not necessarily a reference to the twelve apostles, nor even to committed believers and followers; it can refer to someone who is merely following and learning at that moment—without reference to his level of commitment (see, for instance, Matt. 8:21; or the example of Judas Iscariot). Moreover, if "disciples" are sometimes distinguished from "the crowds" (as in Matt. 23:1), we may be sure that crowds often pressed in close to hear the teaching primarily designed for those most concerned to learn. From the huge crowds assembling from all over northern Palestine, perhaps a smaller crowd of "disciples" followed Jesus to the quiet hill country west of Galilee in order to receive more extended teaching; and perhaps more and more joined the class, partly because of Jesus' rising reputation and partly because a crowd attracts a crowd. This way of understanding the text is confirmed by Matthew's conclusion to the Sermon on the Mount: "When Jesus had finished saying these things, *the crowds* were amazed at his teaching" (7:28). It is confirmed, too, by the fact that Jesus presses these "disciples" to enter the kingdom, to enter into life (7:13f.; 7:21-23).

Jesus arrived at his chosen theatre and "sat down." In his day, this was the traditional position for a teacher in a synagogue or school. Some English versions then say: "He opened his mouth and taught them, saying. . . ." We might ask ourselves wryly how he could have taught them without opening his mouth, until we recognize that the expression is a semitic idiom, a traditional formula. It seems to add deliberateness and sobriety to what follows.

THE NORMS OF THE KINGDOM
Matthew 5:3-12

The Beatitudes, 5:3-10

There are some general observations to make about these beatitudes before examining them individually. First, the word "beatitude" is a rough transliteration of the Latin *beatus*. Some Christians call these beatitudes "macarisms." This is a rough transliteration of the Greek word *makarios*. Both "beatitude" and "macarism" are transliterations of foreign words which can best be translated "blessed."

Although some modern translations prefer "happy" to "blessed," it is a poor exchange. Those who are blessed will generally be profoundly happy; but blessedness cannot be reduced to happiness. In the Scriptures, man can bless God and God can bless man. This duality gives us a clue just what is meant. To be "blessed" means, fundamentally, to be approved, to find approval. When man blesses God, he is approving God. Of course, he is not doing this in some condescending manner, but rather he is eulogizing God, praising God. When God blesses man, he is approving man; and that is always an act of condescension.

Since this is God's universe there can be no higher "blessing" than to be approved by God. We must ask ourselves whose blessing we diligently seek. If God's blessing means more to us than the approval of loved ones no matter how cherished, or of colleagues no matter how influential, then the beatitudes will speak to us very personally and deeply.

Another observation is that the kind of blessing is not arbitrary in any of these eight beatitudes. The thing promised in each case grows naturally (or rather, supernaturally) out of the character described. For example, in verse six the person who hungers and thirsts for righteousness is filled (with righteousness); in verse seven the merciful are shown mercy. The blessing is always correlated with the condition, as we shall see.

Finally, we need to notice that two of the beatitudes promise the same reward. The first beatitude reads, "Blessed are the poor in spirit, for theirs is the kingdom of heaven" (5:3). The last one says, "Blessed are those who are persecuted because of righteousness, for theirs is the kingdom of heaven" (5:10). To begin and end with the same expression is a stylistic device called an "inclusion." This means that everything bracketed between the two can really be included under the one theme, in this case, the kingdom of heaven. That is why I have called the beatitudes, collectively, "The Norms of the Kingdom."

- Poverty of spirit -

First: "Blessed are the poor in spirit, for theirs is the kingdom of heaven" (5:3).

What is poverty of spirit? It is surely not financial destitution, or material poverty. Nor is it poverty of spiritual awareness. Still less is it poor-spiritedness, that is, a deficiency of vitality or courage. And certainly the expression does not denote poverty of Holy Spirit.

The expression seems to have developed in Old Testament times. God's people were often referred to as "the poor" or "the poor of the Lord," owing to their extreme economic distress. This distress often came about because of oppression. Some of the various Hebrew words for "poor" can also mean "lowly," or "humble": the association of the two ideas is natural enough. For example, in Proverbs 16:19 we read, "It is better to be of a humble spirit with the lowly, than to divide the spoil with the proud." The word translated "lowly" is elsewhere rendered "poor"; and both "poor" and "lowly" fit the context. Two verses in Isaiah stand close in meaning to the poverty of spirit of which Jesus speaks: "Thus says the high and lofty One who inhabits eternity, whose name is Holy: I dwell in the high and holy place, and with him also who is of a contrite and humble spirit" (Isa. 57:15). Again: "To this man will I look, namely to him who is poor and of a contrite spirit, and who trembles at my word" (Isa. 66:2).

Poverty of spirit is the personal acknowledgment of spiritual bankruptcy. It is the conscious confession of unworth before God. As such, it is the deepest form of repentance. It is exemplified by the guilty publican in the corner of the Temple: "God, be merciful to me, a sinner!" It is not a man's confession that he is ontologically insignificant, or personally without value, for such would be untrue; it is, rather, a confession that he is sinful and rebellious and utterly without moral virtues adequate to commend him to God. From within such a framework, poverty of spirit becomes a general confession of a man's need for God, a humble admission of impotence without him. Poverty of spirit may *end* in a Gideon vanquishing the enemy hosts; but it *begins* with a Gideon who first affirms he is incapable of the task, and who insists that if the Lord does not go with him he would much prefer to stay home and thresh grain.

Poverty of spirit cannot be artificially induced by self-hatred. Still less does it have in common with showy humility. It cannot be aped successfully by the spiritually haughty who covet its qualities. Such efforts may achieve token success before peers; they never deceive God. Indeed, most of us are repulsed by sham humility, whether our own or that of others.

I suspect that there is no pride more deadly than that which finds its roots in great learning, great external piety, or a showy defense of orthodoxy. My suspicion does not call into question the value of learning, piety, or orthodoxy; rather, it exposes professing believers to the full glare of this beatitude. Pride based on genuine virtues has the greatest potential for self-deception; but our Lord will allow none of it. Poverty of spirit he insists on—a full, honest, factual, conscious, and conscientious recognition before God of personal moral unworth. It is, as I have said, the deepest form of repentance.

It is not surprising, then, that the kingdom of heaven belongs to the poor in spirit. At the very outset of the Sermon on the Mount, we learn that we do not have the spiritual resources to put any of the Sermon's precepts into practice. We cannot fulfill God's standards ourselves. We must come to him and acknowledge our spiritual bankruptcy, emptying ourselves of our self-righteousness, moral self-esteem, and personal vainglory. Emptied of these things we are ready for him to fill us. Much of the rest of the Sermon on the Mount is designed to remove these self-delusions from us, and foster within us a genuine poverty of spirit. The genuineness and depth of this repentance is a prime requirement for entering into life.

> *Second:* "Blessed are those who mourn, for they will be comforted" (5:4).

This verse follows naturally from the one which precedes it. Mournfulness can be understood as the emotional counterpart to poverty of spirit.

The world in which we live likes to laugh. Pleasure dispensers sell cheers and chuckles, all for a neat profit. The *summum bonum* of life becomes a good time, and the immediate goal is the next high. The world does not like mourners; mourners are wet blankets.

Yet the Son of God insists, "Blessed are those who mourn, for they will be comforted." This does not mean the Christian is to be perpetually morose, forever weepy. The Christian must not fit the stereotype in the mind of the little girl who exclaimed, "That horse must be a Christian; it's got such a long face!" Still less is the verse a defense of that grief which arises out of groveling self-pity.

What is it, then? At the individual level, this mourning is a personal grief over personal sin. This is the mourning experienced by a man who begins to recognize the blackness of his sin, the more he is exposed to the purity of God. Isaiah was one such, as he was accorded a vision of the Deity, in which even the very angels of heaven covered their faces and cried in solemn worship, "Holy! Holy! Holy!" Isaiah's reaction was utter devastation (Isa. 6:5). It is the cry of a man who goes after purity in his own strength and finds he cannot achieve it, and cries, "What a wretched man I am! Who will rescue me from this body of death?" (Rom. 7:24).

But there can also be a mourning stimulated by broader consider- ations. Sometimes the sin of this world, the lack of integrity, the injus- tice, the cruelty, the cheapness, the selfishness, all pile onto the consciousness of a sensitive man and make him weep. Most of us would prefer merely to condemn. We are prepared to walk with Jesus through Matthew 23 and repeat his pronouncements of doom; but we stop before we get to the end of the chapter and join him in weeping over the city. The great lights in church history learned to weep—men of the caliber of Calvin, Whitefield, Wesley, Shaftesbury, and Wilberforce.

The Christian is to be the truest realist. He reasons that death is there, and must be faced. God is there, and will be known by all as Sav- ior or Judge. Sin is there, and it is unspeakably ugly and black in the light of God's purity. Eternity is there, and every living human being is rushing toward it. God's revelation is there, and the alternatives it presents will come to pass: life or death, pardon or condemnation, heaven or hell. These are realities which will not go away. The man who lives in the light of them, and rightly assesses himself and his world in the light of them, cannot but mourn. He mourns for the sins and blas- phemies of his nation. He mourns for the erosion of the very concept of truth. He mourns over the greed, the cynicism, the lack of integrity. He mourns that there are so few mourners.

But he will be comforted! And what comfort. There is no comfort or joy that can compare with what God gives to those who mourn. These people exchange the sackcloth of mourning for a garment of praise, the ashes of grief for the oil of gladness. At the individual level, the mourner grieves over his sin because he sees how great is the offense before God; but he learns to trust Jesus as the one who has paid sin's ransom (Mark 10:45). He luxuriates in deep joy as he discovers in his own experience that Jesus came to save His people from their sins (Matt. 1:21). And as he weeps for other men, he finds to his delight that God is answering his prayers, very often even working through him to untangle sin's knots and provide others with new birth, new righteousness. But even this great comfort will be surpassed: one day in a new heaven and new earth, the kingdom of God will be consummated, and God himself will wipe away all tears from the eyes of those who once mourned. There will be no more death or mourning or crying or pain, for the old order of things will have passed away (Rev. 21:4).

Third: "Blessed are the meek, for they will inherit the earth" (5:5).

- meekness -

How does meekness differ from poverty of spirit? In this way, I think: Poverty of spirit has to do with a person's assessment of himself, especially with respect to God, while meekness has more to do with his relationship with God and with men.

Meekness is not, as many people imagine, a weakness. It must not be confused with being wishy-washy. A meek person is not necessarily indecisive or timid. He is not so unsure of himself that he could be pushed over by a hard slap from a wet noodle. Still less is meekness to be confused with mere affability. Some people are just naturally nice and easygoing; but then again, so are some dogs. Meekness goes much deeper.

Meekness is a controlled desire to see the other's interests advance ahead of one's own. Think of Abraham's deference to Lot: that was meekness. According to Numbers 12:3, Moses was the meekest man who ever lived, and his meekness is supremely demonstrated in that chapter by his refusal to defend himself, by his controlled self-commitment to the Lord when his person and privilege were under attack. But it is Jesus himself who is the only one who could ever say with integrity, "Come to me, all you who are weary and burdened, and I will give you rest. Take my yoke upon you and learn from me, for I am meek and humble in heart, and you will find rest for your souls" (Matt. 11:28f.).

Dr. D. Martyn Lloyd-Jones puts it this way:

> The man who is truly meek is the one who is amazed that God and man can think of him as well as they do and treat him as well as they do. . . . Finally, I would put it like this. We are to leave everything—ourselves, our rights, our cause, our whole future—in the hands of God, and especially so if we feel we are suffering unjustly.[*]

The Scriptures make much of meekness (see II Cor. 10:1; Gal. 5:22f.; Col. 3:12; I Peter 3:15f.; James 1:19-21), and so it is the more appalling that meekness does not characterize more of us who claim to be Christians. Both at the personal level, where we are too often concerned with justifying ourselves rather than with edifying our brother, and at the corporate level, where we are more successful at organizing rallies, institutions, and pressure groups than at extending the kingdom of God, meekness has not been the mark of most Christians for a long time.

To the extent that meekness is practiced among us—to that extent, we may be sure—a crassly materialistic world will oppose it. Materialism argues, "Grab what you can; the strong man comes first and the devil take the hindmost." This is true whether one is on the right or the left of the

---

[*]*Studies in the Sermon on the Mount*, 2 vols. (Grand Rapids: Eerdmans, 1959-60), 1:69-70.

political spectrum. Individually, each man tends to assume, without thinking, that he is at the center of the universe; therefore he relates poorly to the four billion others who are laboring under a similar delusion. But the meek man sees himself and all the others under God. Since he is poor in spirit, he does not think more highly of himself than he ought to. Therefore he is able to relate well to others.

And the meek shall inherit the earth! These words, cited from Psalm 37:11, constitute a devastating contradiction to the philosophical materialism so prevalent in our own day. But this blessing of inheritance is true in at least two ways. First, only the genuinely meek man will be content; his ego is not so inflated that he thinks he must always have more. Besides, in Christ he already sees himself "possessing everything" (II Cor. 6:10; cf. I Cor. 3:21-23). With this eternal perspective in view he can afford to be meek. Moreover, one day he will come into the fullness of his inheritance, when he will find the beatitude fulfilled most literally. Fifty billion trillion years into eternity (if I may speak of eternity in terms of time) God's people will still be rejoicing that this beatitude is literally true. In a new heaven *and earth,* they will be grateful that by grace they learned to be meek during their initial threescore years and ten.

Fourth: "Blessed are those who hunger and thirst for righteousness, for they will be filled" (5:6).

Thorough righteousness is often parodied as some form of obsolete Victorian prudishness, or narrow-minded and vehement legalism. The pursuit of righteousness is not popular even among professing Christians. Many today are prepared to seek other things: spiritual maturity, real happiness, the Spirit's power, effective witnessing skills. Other people chase from preacher to preacher and conference to conference seeking some vague "blessing" from on high. They hunger for spiritual experience, they thirst for the consciousness of God.

But how many hunger and thirst for righteousness?

This is not to argue that the other things are not desirable, but rather that they are not as basic as righteousness. It is with good reason that this is the fourth beatitude. The man marked by poverty of spirit (5:3), who grieves over sin personal and social (5:4), and approaches God and man with meekness (5:5), must also be characterized as hungry and thirsty for righteousness (5:6). It is not that he wants to be a little bit better, still less that he thinks of righteousness as an optional luxury to add to his other graces; rather, he *hungers* and *thirsts* for it. He cannot get along without righteousness; it is as important to him as food and drink.

Most people who read these lines have experienced very little hunger and thirst. I myself am not old enough to have undergone the privations many experienced during the Great Depression or the last world war. However, two or three times during the sixties, when I was a student first at university and then at seminary, I ran out of money and food at the same time. Too proud to ask for help, and wanting to see if God would really supply what I needed, I drank water to keep my stomach from rumbling and carried on as usual. After two or three days I *began* to understand what it is to be hungry.

The norms of the kingdom require that men and women be hungry and thirsty for righteousness. This is so basic to Christian living that Dr. D. Martyn Lloyd-Jones says:

> I do not know of a better test that anyone can apply to himself or herself in this whole matter of the Christian profession than a verse like this. If this verse is to you one of the most blessed statements of the whole of Scripture, you can be quite certain you are a Christian; if it is not, then you had better examine the foundations again.[*]

What is this righteousness which we must thus pursue? In Paul's epistles, "righteousness" can refer to the righteousness of Christ which God reckons to the believer's account, even as God reckons the believer's sin to Jesus Christ. If that were the righteousness here in view, Jesus would be inviting unbelievers to pursue the righteousness God bestows by virtue of Christ's substitutionary death. Some have thought that "righteousness" in Matthew's Gospel refers to the vindication of the downtrodden and the afflicted. Now, however, those who have studied Matthew's use of the term increasingly recognize that "righteousness" here (and also in verses 10 and 20) means a pattern of life in conformity to God's will. Righteousness thus includes within its semantic range all the derivative or specialized meanings, but cannot be reduced to any one of them.

The person who hungers and thirsts for righteousness, then, hungers and thirsts for conformity to God's will. He is not drifting aimlessly in a sea of empty religiosity; still less is he puttering about distracted by inconsequential trivia. Rather, his whole being echoes the prayer of a certain Scottish saint who cried, "O God, make me just as holy as a pardoned sinner can be!" His delight is the Word of God, for where else is God's will, to which he hungers to be conformed, so clearly set forth? He wants to be righteous, not simply because he fears God, but because righteousness has become for him the most eminently desirable thing in the world.

And the result? Those who hunger and thirst for righteousness will be

---

[*]Ibid., 1:74

-mercy.

filled. The context demands that we understand the blessing to mean "will be filled *with righteousness.*" The Lord gives this famished person the desires of his heart.

This does not mean that the person is now so satisfied with the righteousness given him that his hunger and thirst for righteousness are forever vanquished. Elsewhere, Jesus does in fact argue along such lines: "Whoever drinks the water I give him will never thirst. . . . I am the bread of life. He who comes to me will never go hungry, and he who believes in me will never be thirsty" (John 4:14; 6:35). So there is a sense in which we are satisfied with Jesus and all he is and provides. Nevertheless, there is a sense in which we continue to be unsatisfied.

An example from Paul makes this paradox understandable. Paul can testify, "I *know* whom I have believed, and am convinced that he is able to guard what I have entrusted to him for that day" (II Tim. 1:12); but he can also say, "I *want to know* Christ and the power of his resurrection and the fellowship of sharing in his sufferings, becoming like him in his death . . ." (Phil. 3:10). In other words, Paul has come to know Christ, but knowing him, he wants to know him better.

In a similar way, the person who hungers and thirsts for righteousness is blessed by God, and filled; but the righteousness with which he is filled is so wonderful that he hungers and thirsts for more of it. This built-in cycle of growth is easy to understand as soon as we remember that righteousness in this text refers not to obeying some rules, but to conformity to all of God's will. The more a person pursues conformity to God's will, the more attractive the goal becomes, and the greater the advances made.

Fifth: "Blessed are the merciful, for they will be shown mercy" (5:7).

Some try to interpret this verse legalistically, as if to say that the only way to obtain mercy from God is by showing mercy to others: God's mercy thus becomes essentially contingent to our own. They point to Matthew 6:14f. (which we shall consider in the third chapter): "For if you forgive men when they sin against you, your heavenly Father will also forgive you. But if you do not forgive men their sins, your Father will not forgive your sins." But whenever a tit-for-tat interpretation of such verses prevails, I think there is a failure to understand both the context and the nature of mercy.

What is mercy? How does it differ from grace? The two terms are frequently synonymous; but where there is a distinction between the two, it appears that grace is a loving response when love is undeserved, and mercy is a loving response prompted by the misery and helplessness of the one on whom the love is to be showered. Grace answers to the undeserving; mercy answers to the miserable.

Jesus says in this beatitude that we are to be merciful. We are to be compassionate and gentle, especially toward the miserable and helpless. If we are not merciful, we will not be shown mercy. But how could the unmerciful man receive mercy? The one who is not merciful is inevitably so unaware of his own state that he thinks he needs no mercy. He cannot picture himself as miserable and wretched; so how shall God be merciful toward him? He is like the Pharisee in the temple who was unmerciful toward the wretched tax collector in the corner (Luke 18:10ff.). By contrast, the person whose experience reflects these beatitudes is conscious of his spiritual bankruptcy (Matt. 5:3), grieves over it (5:4) and hungers for righteousness (5:6). He is merciful toward the wretched because he recognizes himself to be wretched; in being merciful he is also shown mercy.

The Christian, moreover, is at a mid-point. He is to forgive others because in the past Christ has already forgiven him (cf. Eph. 4:32; Col. 3:13). Simultaneously he recognizes his constant need for more forgiveness, and becomes forgiving as a result of this perspective as well (cf. Matt. 6:14; and especially 18:21-35). The Christian forgives because he has been forgiven; he forgives because he needs forgiveness. In precisely the same way, and for the same kind of reasons, the disciple of Jesus Christ is merciful.

It is sometimes said that an alcoholic who won't admit he's an alcoholic hates all other alcoholics. Similarly, it is generally true that the sinner who won't face up to his sin hates all other sinners. But the person who has recognized his own helplessness and wretchedness is grateful for whatever mercy is shown him; and he learns to be merciful toward others.

This macarism forces the professing disciple of Jesus Christ to ask himself some hard questions. Am I merciful or supercilious to the wretched? Am I gentle or hard-nosed toward the downtrodden? Am I helpful or callous toward the backslidden? Am I compassionate or impatient with the fallen?

I am persuaded that, should the Spirit of God usher in another period of refreshing revival in the Western world, one of the earliest signs of it will be that admission of spiritual bankruptcy which finds its satisfaction in God and his righteousness, and goes on to be richly merciful toward others.

Sixth: "Blessed are the pure in heart, for they will see God" (5:8).

In this beatitude, our Lord confers special blessing not on the intellectually keen, nor on the emotionally pious, but on the pure in heart. In biblical imagery, the heart is the center of the entire personality. Jesus' assessment of the natural heart, however, is not very encouraging. Elsewhere in Matthew's Gospel he says, "For out of the heart come evil thoughts, murder, adultery, sexual immorality, theft, false testimony, slander" (15:19; cf. Jer. 17:9; Rom. 1:21; 2:5).

Despite this horrible diagnosis, the sixth beatitude insists that purity of heart is the indispensable prerequisite for fellowship with God—for "seeing" God. "Who shall ascend into the hill of the Lord? Who shall stand in his holy place? He who has clean hands *and a pure heart*, who has not lifted up his soul to vanity, nor sworn deceitfully" (Ps. 24:3f; cf. Ps. 73:1). God is holy; therefore the writer of the epistle to the Hebrews insists, "Make every effort . . . to be holy; without holiness no one will see the Lord" (Heb. 12:14).

Purity of heart must never be confused with outward conformity to rules. Because it is the heart which must be pure, this beatitude interrogates us with awkward questions like these: What do you think about when your mind slips into neutral? How much sympathy do you have for deception, no matter how skillful? For shady humor, no matter how funny? To what do you pay consistent allegiance? What do you want more than anything else? What and whom do you love? To what extent are your actions and words accurate reflections of what is in your heart? To what extent do your actions and words constitute a cover-up for what is in your heart? Our hearts must be pure, clean, unstained.

One day, when the kingdom of heaven is consummated, when there is a new heaven and a new earth in which only righteousness dwells, when Jesus Christ himself appears, we shall be like him (I John 3:2). That is our long-range expectation, our hope. On this basis John argues, "Everyone who has hope in him [that is, in Christ] purifies himself, just as he is pure" (I John 3:3). In other words, according to John, the Christian purifies himself now because pure is what he will ultimately be. His present efforts are consistent with his future hope. The same theme is found in various forms throughout the New Testament. In one sense, of course, the demands of the kingdom do not change: perfection is always required (5:48). But from this it follows that the disciple of Jesus who looks forward to the kingdom as it will be finally perfected, is already determined to prepare for it. Knowing himself to be in the kingdom already, he is concerned with purity because he recognizes that the King is pure, and the kingdom in its perfected form will admit only purity.

The pure in heart are blessed because they will see God. Although this will not be ultimately true until the new heaven and earth, yet it is also *peacemakers –*

true even now. Our perception of God and his ways, as well as our fellowship with him, depends on our purity of heart. The *visio Dei*—what an incentive to purity!

> *Seventh*: "Blessed are the peacemakers, for they will be called sons of God" (5:9).

This beatitude does not hold out a blessing to the peaceful, nor to those who yearn for peace, but to the peace*makers*.

Within the total biblical framework, the greatest peacemaker is Jesus Christ—the Prince of Peace. He makes peace between God and man by removing sin, the ground of alienation; he makes peace between man and man both by removing sin and by bringing men into a right relationship with God (see especially Eph. 2:11-22). Jesus gave the traditional Jewish greeting new depths of meaning when, *after his death and resurrection*, he greeted his disciples with the words, "Peace be with you" (Luke 24:36; John 20:19). Thus the good news of Jesus Christ is the greatest peacemaking message, and the Christian who shares his faith is, fundamentally, a harbinger of peace, a peacemaker. Small wonder Paul uses the imagery of Isaiah, who pictures messengers racing along the trails of the Judean hill country: "How beautiful on the mountains are the feet of those who bring good news, who proclaim peace, who bring good tidings, who proclaim salvation, who say to Zion, 'Your God reigns!'" (Isa. 52:7; Rom. 10:15).

Yet there is nothing in the context to argue that in Matthew 5:9 Jesus is restricting himself to gospel peacemaking. Rather, the disciple of Jesus Christ must be a peacemaker in the broadest sense of the term. The Christian's role as peacemaker extends not only to spreading the gospel, but to lessening tensions, seeking solutions, ensuring that communication is understood. Perhaps his most difficult assignments will take place on those occasions when he is personally involved. Then he will remember that "man's anger does not bring about the righteous life that God desires" (James 1:20), and that "a soft answer turns away wrath" (Prov. 15:1). He will not confuse issues, even important issues, with his own ego-image; and fearful lest he be guilty of generating more heat than light, he will learn to lower his voice and smile more broadly in proportion to the intensity of the argument.

Peacemakers are blessed because they will be called "sons of God"—not "children of God," as in the King James Version. The difference is slight, but significant. In Jewish thought, "son" often bears the meaning "partaker of the character of," or the like. If someone calls you the "son of a dog," this is not an aspersion on your parents, but on you:

you partake of the character of a dog. Thus, "son of God" may have a different connotation than "child of God." Both expressions can refer to some sort of filial relationship; but the former has more emphasis on character than position.

The peacemaker's reward, then, is that he will be called a son of God. He reflects his heavenly Father's wonderful peacemaking character. Even now there is a sense in which Christians intuitively recognize this divine dimension in the character of the peacemaker. For example, when Christians at some convention or church business meeting enter into heated debate, the brother who keeps calm, respectfully listens to each viewpoint with fairness and courtesy, and spreads oil on the troubled waters is silently regarded by his peers as spiritual. But such conduct ought to be considered normal among disciples of Jesus Christ, for Jesus Christ himself has made it normative. It is part and parcel of being a son of God.

Eighth: "Blessed are those who are persecuted because of righteousness, for theirs is the kingdom of heaven" (5:10).

This final beatitude does not say, "Blessed are those who are persecuted because they are objectionable, or because they rave like wild-eyed fanatics, or because they pursue some religio-political cause." The blessing is restricted to those who suffer persecution *because of righteousness* (cf. I Peter 3:13f.; 4:12-16). The believers described in this passage are those determined to live as Jesus lived.

Persecution can take many forms; it need not be limited to the rigorous variety experienced by our fellow-believers in certain repressive countries. A Christian in the West who practices righteousness may be ridiculed by his family, ostracized by his relatives. But even the Christian who comes from a secure and understanding home will face flak somewhere. Perhaps at work, he will discover that some of his colleagues are saying of him, "Well, you know, he's a Christian; but he carries it a bit far. He won't even cheat on his income tax. The other day when I offered to slip him a company binder that I knew he needed for his private papers at home, he turned it down. When I pressed him, he said that taking it would be stealing! And have you ever seen his face cloud over when I tell one of my jokes? What a prig!"

The reward for being persecuted because of righteousness is the kingdom of heaven. In other words, this beatitude serves as a test for all the beatitudes. Just as a person must be poor in spirit to enter the kingdom (5:3), so will he be persecuted because of righteousness if he is to enter the kingdom. This final beatitude becomes one of the most searching of all of them, and binds up the rest; for if the disciple of Jesus never experiences any persecution at all, it may fairly be asked where righteousness is being displayed in his life. If there is no righteousness, no conformity to God's will, how shall he enter the kingdom?

This basic principle reappears again and again in the New Testament. The Christian lives in a sinful world; therefore if he exhibits genuine, transparent righteousness he will be rejected by many. Genuine righteousness condemns people by implication; small wonder that people often lash out in retaliation. Christ's disciples by their righteous living thus divide men: men are either repelled or drawn to our precious Savior. Jesus himself taught:

> If the world hates you, keep in mind that it hated me first. If you belonged to the world, it would love you as its own. As it is, you do not belong to the world, but I have chosen you out of the world. That is why the world hates you. Remember the words I spoke to you: "No servant is greater than his master." If they persecuted me, they will persecute you also. If they obeyed my teaching, they will obey yours also (John 15:18-20).

Paul adds, "For it has been granted to you on behalf of Christ not only to believe on him, but also to suffer for him" (Phil. 1:29). "In fact, everyone who wants to live a godly life in Christ Jesus will be persecuted" (II Tim. 3:12; cf. I Thess. 3:3f.).

This eighth beatitude is so important that Jesus expands it, making it more pointed by changing the third person form of the beatitudes to the direct address of second person:

Expansion, 5:11f.

> Blessed are you when people insult you, persecute you and falsely say all kinds of evil against you because of me. Rejoice and be glad, because great is your reward in heaven, for in the same way they persecuted the prophets who were before you (5:11f.).

Besides the impact of the direct discourse, this expansion of the eighth beatitude affords three important insights.

First, persecution is explicitly broadened to include insults and spoken malice. It cannot be limited to physical opposition or torture.

Second, the phrase "because of righteousness" (5:10) Jesus now parallels with "because of me" (5:11). This confirms that the righteousness of life that is in view is in imitation of Jesus. Simultaneously, it so identifies the disciple of Jesus with the practice of Jesus' righteousness that there is no place for professed allegiance to Jesus that is not full of righteousness.

Third, there is an open command to rejoice and be glad when suffering under persecution of this type. Elsewhere in the New Testament, many different reasons are advanced for rejoicing under persecution. The apostles rejoiced "because they had been counted worthy of suffering disgrace for the Name" (Acts 5:41). Peter saw trials as a means of grace to prove the genuineness of faith and to increase its purity (I Peter 1:6ff.). And in the Old Testament the fiery furnace became the place where the divine Presence, even in a visible emissary, was made manifest to three Hebrew young men (Dan. 3:24f.). However, in the passage before us only one reason is given to prompt Jesus' disciples to rejoice under persecution, and that reason is sufficient: their reward is great in heaven. Jesus' disciples, then, must determine their values from the perspective of eternity (a theme Jesus expands in Matt. 6:19-21, 33), convinced that their "light and momentary troubles are achieving for [them] an eternal glory that far outweighs them all" (II Cor. 4:17). They have aligned themselves with the prophets who were persecuted before them, and thereby testify that in every age God's people are under the gun. Far from being a depressing prospect, their suffering under persecution, which has been prompted by their righteousness, becomes a triumphant sign that the kingdom is theirs.

THE WITNESS OF THE KINGDOM
Matthew 5:13-16

These verses are tied to the preceding ones in two ways. First, Jesus continues to address his hearers in the second person. Second, and more important, a motif implicit in the beatitudes now becomes an explicit theme, i.e., the believer as witness.

To see how this works out, we must recognize that it is impossible to follow the norms of the kingdom in a purely private way. The righteousness of the life you live will attract attention, even if that attention regularly takes the form of opposition. In other words, the Christian is not poor in spirit, mournful over sin, meek, hungry and thirsty for righteousness, merciful, pure in heart, a peacemaker—all in splendid isolation. These kingdom norms, diligently practised in a sinful world, constitute a major aspect of Christian witness; and this witness gives rise to persecution. Nevertheless, the conduct of Jesus' disciples needs to be considered in its effect on the world, just as the opposition of the world has been considered in its effect on the Christian. In verses 13-16, therefore, Jesus develops two telling metaphors to picture how his disciples must by their lives leave their stamp on the world which is so opposed to the norms of the kingdom.

Salt, 5:13

In the ancient world, salt was used primarily as a preservative. Since they did not own deep-freeze refrigerators, the people used salt to preserve many foodstuffs. Incidentally, of course, salt also helps the flavor.

In the first metaphor Jesus likens his disciples to salt. Implicitly he is saying that apart from his disciples the world turns ever more rotten: Christians have the effect of delaying moral and spiritual putrefaction. If their lives conform to the norms of verses 3-12, they cannot help but be an influence for good in society.

But supposing the salt loses its saltiness? What then? It loses its *raison d'être*, and may just as well be thrown out onto the street—the garbage dump of the ancient east—to be trampled by men.

This observation has been interpreted two ways. Because salt by its nature cannot be anything other than salt, it cannot really lose its saltiness; therefore some have taken Jesus to be saying that there is an inner necessity which compels Christians to witness. This interpretation, it seems to me, smacks of the pedantic. Although salt *per se* cannot lose its saltiness, it can nevertheless be adulterated. If sufficiently adulterated by, say, sand, then salt can no longer be used as a preservative. It loses its effectiveness in staying corruption, and so must be jettisoned as a useless commodity. The purpose of salt is to fight deterioration, and therefore it must not itself deteriorate.

The worse the world becomes and the more its corruption proceeds apace, the more it stands in need of Jesus' disciples.

Light, 5:14-16

The second metaphor our Lord uses to describe the witness of the Christian is light. Christians are the light of the world—a world which, by implication, is shrouded in thick darkness.

Jesus talks about two sources of physical light: the light from a city set on a hill, and the light from a lamp set on a lampstand. The first source, the city, is often misunderstood. Some think that Matthew, in recording Jesus' teaching, became somewhat confused and put in an irrelevant illustration about a city visible from a great distance because of its elevation. The illustration is colorful, it is thought, but out of place in a context concerned with light. Such critics, I think, are only revealing that they live in the industrialized world where light is so readily available. They do not know how black nature can be. In Canada it is possible to go camping hundreds of miles away from any city or town. If it is a cloudy night, and there is no phosphorus in the area, the blackness is total. A hand held three inches from your face cannot be seen. But if there is a city nearby, perhaps a hundred miles away, the darkness is relieved. The light from the city is reflected off the clouds, and the night, once perfectly black, is no longer quite so desolate. Likewise Christians who let their light shine before men cannot be hidden; and the good light they shed around attenuates the blackness which would otherwise be absolute.

When once we imagine a world without hundreds of watts of electric power at our instant personal disposal, we will understand how darkness can be a terror and a symbol of all that is evil. The light from the city, even if it is not as powerful as our modern sources of illumination, makes the darkness a little more bearable than it was before. Light is so important that it is ludicrous to think that anyone would want to extinguish the flickering flame from an olive-oil lamp by smothering it with a peck measure. That burning wick may cast only a little light by modern standards; but if the alternative is pitch blackness, its light is wonderful, quite sufficient for everyone in the house (5:15).

"In the same way, let your light shine before men, that they may see your good deeds and praise your Father in heaven" (5:16). What is this light by which Jesus' disciples lighten a dark world? In this context, we read of neither personal confrontation nor ecclesiastical pronouncement. Rather, the light is the "good deeds" performed by Jesus' followers—performed in such a way that at least some men recognize these followers of Jesus as sons of God, and come to praise this Father whose sons they are (5:16).

The norms of the kingdom, worked out in the lives of the heirs of the kingdom, constitute the witness of the kingdom. Such Christians refuse to rob their employers by being lazy on the job, or to rob their employees by succumbing to greed and stinginess. They are first to help a colleague in difficulty, last to return a barbed reply. They honestly desire the advancement of the other's interests, and honestly dislike smutty humor. Transparent in their honesty and genuine in their concern, they reject both the easy answer of the doctrinaire politician and the *laissez-faire* stance of the selfish secular man. Meek in personal demeanor, they are bold in righteous pursuits.

For a variety of reasons, Christians have lost this vision of witness, and are slow to return to it. But in better days and other lands, the faithful and divinely empowered proclamation of the gospel of Jesus Christ (who himself is the light of the world *par excellence* [John 8:12]) so transformed men that they in turn became the light of the world (Matt. 5:14). Prison reform, medical care, trade unions, control of a perverted and perverting liquor trade, abolition of slavery, abolition of child labor, establishment of orphanages, reform of the penal code—in all these areas the followers of Jesus spearheaded the drive for righteousness.* The darkness was alleviated. And this, I submit, has always been the pattern when professing Christians have been less concerned with personal prestige and more concerned with the norms of the kingdom.

"In the same way, let your light shine before men, that they may see your good deeds and praise your Father in heaven."

---

*I recommend the reading of such books as J. W. Bready's *England: Before and After Wesley* (in the abridged American edition, the title is *This Freedom—Whence?*), or D. W. Dayton's more recent *Discovering an Evangelical Heritage.* Although I am not always convinced by their theological analyses, nevertheless such books teach us how almost all valuable social trends were spawned by the Evangelical Awakening under such men of God as George Whitefield, John Wesley, Howell Harris, Lord Shaftesbury, William Wilberforce, and others.

2 MATTHEW 5:17-47

THE KINGDOM OF HEAVEN:
Its Demands in Relation to the Old Testament

We are sometimes in danger of treating God's Word as if it were a collection of loose, unclassified gems. The Bible then becomes a mere sourcebook of "precious thoughts." When it is handled in this way, many important things are lost to view: the historical development of God's redemptive purposes; his people's increased theological understanding as he progressively reveals himself and his ways; the literary structure which binds together a book or a discourse into coherent themes and sub-themes. On the other hand, when these historical, theological, and literary factors are properly considered, they contribute in important ways to our understanding of each part of the Bible—not. least of all the Sermon on the Mount.

Take for example the literary structure. The kingdom of heaven is an important theme in Matthew's Gospel, and we have already noted how, by the literary device of an inclusion (5:3, 10), it becomes central in the beatitudes. Moreover, the first sixteen verses of Matthew 5 introduce or anticipate all the main themes of Matthew 5—7 in such a way as to provoke the reader to self-examination and arouse his interest in what follows. These chapters end with a number of contrasts, demanding that we choose one of two paths, one of two trees, one of two claims, one of two foundations (7:13-27). Between the introduction (5:3-16) of the Sermon on the Mount and its conclusion (7:13-27) is the body of it (5:17—7:12). This body is bracketed by another inclusion, i.e., the Law and the Prophets (5:17; 7:12), a common way of referring to the Old Testament Scriptures. So in studying 5:17-48, we recognize two things: first, we are entering the great body of the Sermon; and second, Jesus is taking pains to relate his teaching to the Old Testament.

Of course, we might have expected this emphasis on the Old Testament from our reading of the introduction, the first sixteen verses; for there Jesus says that those who practise the norms of the kingdom and therefore bear witness to the kingdom will not only enjoy great reward in heaven but will find themselves *aligned with the prophets* (5:12).

Thus, from predominantly literary considerations we are plunged into major themes which raise important historical and theological questions. The Sermon on the Mount promises not only to give us some challenging thoughts about poverty of spirit, righteousness, love, forgiveness, and the like, but also promises to reveal something of the way Jesus himself sees his place in history, the relationship between his kingdom-preaching and the Old Testament Scriptures.

Moreover, if we understand that Jesus taught as a first-century Jew to first-century Jews, we shall expect his teaching to be framed in categories comprehensible primarily to his audience, and aimed at least in part at correcting first-century impressions and beliefs which he considered erroneous. This observation grounds the revelation of God through Jesus Christ *in history*, and, as we shall see, enhances our understanding of the Sermon on the Mount.

JESUS AS FULFILLMENT
OF THE OLD TESTAMENT
Matthew 5:17-20

Matthew 5:17-20 are among the most difficult verses in all the Bible. Superficially it is clear what they are about. Jesus again picks up the theme of the kingdom (mentioned three times in 5:19f.) and now relates it to the Law and the Prophets. These verses then serve as the introduction to the five blocks of material which make up the rest of the chapter.

It is also clear that Matthew 5:17f. portrays Jesus' high view of what we call the Old Testament Scriptures. Jesus did not come to abolish these writings; rather, he acknowledges their immutability right down to the smallest letter, the "jot," or right down to the least stroke of the pen. This least stroke, the "tittle" (KJV), is what we would call a serif, the tiny extension on some letters that distinguishes older type faces from more modern ones. In Hebrew this tiny extension is needed to differentiate between several pairs of letters. Jesus is therefore upholding the reliability and truthfulness of the written text. He is not merely saying that the Old Testament contains some truth, still less that it becomes true when men encounter it meaningfully. Rather, as he says elsewhere, the Scripture cannot be broken (John 10:35).*

These observations also bring us into difficulty. If Jesus did not see himself abolishing the Law and the Prophets, but fulfilling them, why, for example, is there good evidence that he abolished the food laws (Mark 7:19)? Why do New Testament writers, after Jesus' death and resurrection, insist that the sacrificial system of the Old Testament is at best no longer necessary, and in principle abolished (see Heb. 8:13; 10:1-18)? Why do not Christians today try to follow the detailed Old Testament law?

Various answers have been put forward. At least as far back as Thomas Aquinas (c. 1225-74), many Christians have divided the law into three categories: moral, civil, and ceremonial. Some say that the civil law of the Old Testament has passed away because God's people today no longer constitute a nation. The ceremonial law has disappeared because it pointed to Jesus, who "fulfilled" it by dying on the cross, thereby rendering the Old Testament ceremonies obsolete. That leaves the moral law; and, it is argued, Jesus in Matthew 5:17-20 is actually referring only to moral law, which never changes.

The first problem with that view is that the expression "not the smallest letter, not the least stroke of a pen" (5:18) sounds much more all-embracing than would be allowed by an exclusive reference to moral law. Moreover, neither the Old nor the New Testaments utilize this three-fold distinction. Of course, that fact by itself is not conclusive: many legitimate distinctions may be deduced from Scripture even though they may not be explicitly taught.

The problem with this three-fold division is that it's not clear what "moral" then means. If it has to do with what is fundamentally right or wrong, I would want to argue that what God approves is fundamentally right and what he forbids is fundamentally wrong; and in that case, when God approved certain ceremonial sacrifices in the Old Testament, people were *morally* bound to practice them. Again, if God forbade certain *civil* practices in the Old Testament, it would have been *immoral* to proceed with them, just because it was God who prohibited them. So this definition of "moral" runs into problems if the three-fold division— moral, ceremonial, civil—is adopted. The three categories are not sufficiently mutually exclusive. If on the other hand moral law refers to what God *always* approves, then we still face two difficulties: (1) If Jesus in 5:18 is arguing that only moral law never changes, he is arguing in a circle: i.e., "Only law which God always approves (and which therefore

---

*A book which very helpfully sets out Jesus' view of the Old Testament has been written by J. W. Wenham. It is called *Christ and the Bible* (Inter-Varsity Press).

never changes) never changes." (2) Alternatively, if Jesus means to *establish* this definition of moral law, it is odd that he should use such inclusive language (5:18). Appeal to the historic three-fold division of law undoubtedly has merit in certain contexts; but I don't think it helps us explain what Jesus means in Matthew 5:17ff.

Another common approach to this passage is the suggestion that "to fulfill" here means something like "to confirm." Jesus himself fulfilled the law by keeping it perfectly; and now he fulfills it in the lives of his followers by means of his Spirit: Romans 8:4 says that God sent his Son "in order that the righteous requirements of the law might be fully met in us, who do not live according to our sinful nature but according to the Spirit." In this sense, it is argued, what the law really means is confirmed by the lives of both Jesus and his disciples. These points are, no doubt, true; but they do not appear to be taught here. The language of verse 18 seems tighter than that.

Many commentators argue that Christ fulfills the law and the prophets in two different ways. The prophets are fulfilled by Jesus in a predictive fashion: what they predict comes to pass and is thereby fulfilled. The law, however, is not predictive, and is fulfilled in some other way. Some say it is fulfilled in the sense argued above—i.e., it is confirmed in its deeper meaning. Others say Jesus fulfilled the law by dying on the cross, thus satisfying the demands of the law against all who would believe in him.

I am sure all of these ideas find support elsewhere in the New Testament; but are any of them convincing in this context? Do they conform with the way Matthew uses words, or with the motifs Matthew emphasizes?

Over the years a somewhat different approach has been suggested from time to time, and I think it has much to commend it. Elsewhere Matthew records Jesus as saying, "From the days of John the Baptist until now, the kingdom of heaven has been forcefully advancing, and forceful men lay hold of it. For *all the Prophets and the Law prophesied* until John" (Matt. 11:12f.). Not only do the Prophets prophesy, but the Law prophesies. The entire Old Testament has a prophetic function; and Jesus came to fulfill the Old Testament.

However, to understand how he fulfills the Old Testament, we must understand how it prophesies. Some of it is prophecy in the simple predictive sense; and, from the New Testament perspective, it is clear that the Old Testament prophecies focused on the Messiah. For example, the place of his birth is foretold (Mic. 5:2; Matt. 2:5f.). But some Old Testament prophecies cited by Matthew are not nearly so clear. For example, Hosea 11:1, "I called my son out of Egypt," is used to point toward Jesus' return from Egypt to Palestine after the death of Herod the Great (Matt. 2:15); but originally it referred to the exodus of the Is-raelites under Moses. It appears, in this case, that it is the history of the Jews which points forward to Christ, but not in any easy predictive sense.

There are many hints in Matthew's Gospel that this form of "prophecy" is not uncommon. Thus, if in Deuteronomy 8 Moses reminds the people that they wandered for forty years in the desert, where God permitted them to suffer hunger in order that they might learn that man does not live on bread alone, so also Jesus endured hunger for forty days in the desert, and when tempted to doubt God's provision replied that "man does not live on bread alone, but on every word that comes from the mouth of God" (Matt. 4:1-4). This quotation is from the Pentateuch (Deut. 8:2f.), what the Jews called the Law in the narrow sense, and some prophetic function is here presupposed for it.

The New Testament interprets the Old as pointing forward to Christ and the blessings he brings. For example, the sacrificial system pointed toward Jesus' sacrifice (Heb. 9:8f.; 10:1f.). Indeed everything had to be *fulfilled* that was written about Christ in the Law of Moses, the Prophets, and the Psalms (Luke 24:44), and therefore the resurrected Lord could explain to his disciples what was said in all the Scriptures concerning himself—beginning with Moses and all the Prophets (Luke 24:27). The Scriptures testify about him (John 5:39).

In Matthew 5:17f., therefore, we must rid ourselves of conceptions of fulfillment which are too narrow. Jesus fulfills the entire Old Testa-ment—the Law and the Prophets—in many ways. Because they point toward him, he has certainly not come to abolish them. Rather, he has come to fulfill them in a rich diversity of ways, a richness barely hinted at in these paragraphs. Not a single item of the Law or the Prophets shall fail, says Jesus: not ever, until heaven and earth disappear—until everything is accomplished. The clause "until heaven and earth disap-pear" simply means "never, till the end of time"; but it is qualified by the further clause, "until everything is accomplished."

In other words, Jesus does not conceive of his life and ministry in terms of *opposition* to the Old Testament, but in terms of *bringing to fruition* that toward which it points. Thus, the Law and the Prophets, far from being abolished, find their valid continuity in terms of their out-working in Jesus. The detailed prescriptions of the Old Testament may well be superseded, because whatever is prophetic must be in some sense provisional. But whatever is prophetic likewise discovers its legiti-mate continuity in the happy arrival of that toward which it has pointed.

All this presupposes that a fresh approach to the Old Testament is being inaugurated by Jesus, concomitant with the transformed perspec-tive brought about by the advance of the kingdom. Indeed, Jesus himself later teaches just that. He says, "Therefore every teacher of the law who has been instructed about the kingdom of heaven is like the owner of a house who brings out of his storeroom new treasures as well as old" (Matt. 13:52).

In the passage previously cited from Matthew 11:12f., we observe further that the Law and the Prophets exercise this prophetic function until John the Baptist. From John the Baptist on, the kingdom of heaven advances (cf. also Luke 16:16f., where the expression is "kingdom of God"). Similarly, in the next two verses of Matthew 5 (19, 20), Jesus moves on from talking about the Law and the Prophets to talking about the kingdom: "Anyone who breaks one of the least of these commandments and teaches others to do the same will be called least in the kingdom of heaven, but whoever practises and teaches these commands will be called great in the kingdom of heaven." The expression "these commands" does not, I think, refer to the commands of the Old Testament law. It refers, rather, to the commands of the kingdom of heaven, the kingdom mentioned three times in verses 19f. They are the commands already given, and the commands still to come, in the Sermon on the Mount.

Some have thought that the Jews expected new law when the Messiah came. I disagree. The flow of the argument in this passage points in a slightly different direction. It runs something like this: Jesus came not to abolish the Old Testament but to fulfill it—fulfill it in the sense that he himself was the object toward which it pointed. Therefore it is the height of folly not to listen to his commands, the commands of the kingdom. (For a similar argument, see Heb. 2:1-3.) What is required is a "righteousness [which] surpasses that of the Pharisees and the teachers of the law" (5:20), for otherwise there is no entrance into the kingdom of heaven. Indeed, even ranking within the kingdom is dependent on obedience to Jesus' commands (5:19); but that is not surprising when we remember the tremendous emphasis which the Sermon on the Mount places on obedience to Jesus (cf. Matt. 7:21-23), or Jesus' repeated refrain, "But I tell you" (see Matt. 5:20, 22, 26, 28, 32, 34, 39, 44). The Old Testament pointed to the Messiah and the kingdom he would introduce; Jesus, claiming to fulfill that Old Testament anticipation, introduces the kingdom to his followers. In doing so, he stresses obedience and surpassing righteousness, without which there is no admittance. It is worth noting that Jesus' closing words in Matthew's Gospel again emphasize obedience: the believers are to make disciples of all nations, baptizing them and teaching them *to obey everything Jesus has commanded* (28:18-20). Jesus' commands are highlighted, much as in 5:19.

By now it is clear that the Sermon on the Mount is not soporific sentimentality designed to induce a kind of feeble-minded do-goodism. Nor do these chapters tolerate the opinion that Jesus' views on righteousness have been so tempered with love that righteousness slips to a lower level than when its standard was dictated by law. Instead, we discover that the righteousness demanded by Jesus surpasses anything imagined by the Pharisees, the strict orthodox religious group of Jesus' day. Christ's way is more challenging and more demanding—as well as more rewarding—than any legal system can ever be. Moreover, his way was prophetically indicated before it actually arrived; as Paul says, "But now a righteousness from God, apart from the law, has been made known, to which *the Law and the Prophets testify*" (Rom. 3:21).

Thus, by another route we have returned to the inner purity described in the beatitudes. Just as the beatitudes make poverty of spirit a necessary condition for entrance into the kingdom, so Matthew 5:17-20 ends up demanding a kind of righteousness which must have left Jesus' hearers gasping in dismay and conscious of their own spiritual bankruptcy. By this means the Sermon on the Mount lays the foundation of the New Testament doctrines of justification by grace through faith, and sanctification by the regenerating work of the Holy Spirit. Small wonder Paul, that most faultless of Pharisees (Phil. 3:4-6), when he came to understand the Gospel of Christ, considered his spiritual assets rubbish. His new desire was to gain Christ, not having a righteousness of his own that comes from the law, but one which is from God and by faith in Christ (Phil. 3:8f.).

APPLICATION
Matthew 5:21-47

With matchless authority, Jesus has made himself the pivotal point of history. The Old Testament points toward him; and now, having arrived, he introduces the kingdom and shows how the Old Testament finds its ultimate validity and real continuity in himself and his teaching.

At the same time, Jesus must contend with another problem. He cannot assume that everything the people have heard concerning the content of the Old Testament Scriptures was really in the Old Testament. This is because the Pharisees and teachers of the law regarded certain oral traditions as equal in authority with the Scripture itself, thereby contaminating the teaching of Scripture with some fallacious but tenaciously-held interpretations. Therefore in each of the five blocks of material which follow, Jesus says something like this: "You have heard that it was said . . . but I tell you. . . ." He does not begin these contrasts by telling them what the Old Testament said, but what they had heard it said. This is an important observation, because Jesus is not negating something from the Old Testament, but something from their understanding of it.

In other words, Jesus appears to be concerned with two things: overthrowing erroneous traditions, and indicating authoritatively the real direction toward which the Old Testament Scriptures point.

Vilifying anger and reconciliation, 5:21-26

The people had heard that it was said to their ancestors, "Do not murder, and anyone who murders will be subject to judgment." The explicit prohibition was the sixth of the ten commandments; the threat of judgment was part of the Mosaic legislation dealing with murder. The person who murdered someone had to appear before a court and be judged.

But is murder merely an action, committed without reference to the character of the murderer? Is not something more fundamental at stake, namely his view of other people (his victim or victims included)? Does not the murderer's wretched anger and spiteful wrath lurk in the black shadows behind the deed itself? And does not this fact mean that the anger and wrath are themselves blameworthy? Jesus therefore insists that not only the murderer, but anyone who is angry with his brother, will be subject to judgment.

Several observations are in order. First, some early manuscripts of the New Testament add the words "without cause" after "angry with his brother": i.e., "But I tell you that anyone who is angry with his brother *without cause* will be subject to judgment." These words are almost certainly a later addition. Some scribe no doubt thought Jesus couldn't possibly have been so rigid as to exclude all anger, and inserted the words to soften the statement.

Second, this categorical and antithetical way of speaking is typical of much of Jesus' preaching, and reflects, I think, a semitic and poetic cast of mind. It is something we shall wrestle with repeatedly in the Sermon on the Mount; but it is also found elsewhere. For example, in Luke 14:26, Jesus says, "If anyone comes to me and does not hate his father and mother, his wife and children, his brothers and sisters—yes, even his own life—he cannot be my disciple." "Hate" is not to be taken absolutely. Jesus is saying rather that love and allegiance must be given in a preeminent way to himself alone; rivals must not be allowed to usurp what is not their due. But Jesus says it in this antithetical fashion (cf. Matt. 10:37), even though elsewhere he upholds the importance, for example, of honoring parents (Mark 7:10ff.). And indeed, it is important to let this antithetical and categorical form of statement speak, in all its stark absoluteness, before we allow it to be tempered by broader considerations. In Matthew 5:21ff., Jesus relates anger to murder: let that relationship stand before going on to observe that some anger, including anger in Jesus' own life, is not only justifiable but good. Of this I shall say more later.

Third, if anger is forbidden, so also is contempt. "Raca" is an Aramaic expression of abuse. It means "empty," and could perhaps be translated "you blockhead!" or the like. Again, no one may say to another, "You fool!"

People who indulge in actions and attitudes of this type are subject to judgement, to the Sanhedrin, to Gehenna. The Sanhedrin was the highest Jewish court in the land. "Gehenna" is a Greek transliteration of two semitic words which mean "Valley of Hinnom," a ravine south of Jerusalem where rubbish was dumped and burned, and which consequently became a euphemism for "the fire of hell."

Some have tried to see in these three steps—anger, "Raca," "You fool!"—a gradation; but it is difficult to believe that Jesus is stooping to such casuistry. Would he resort to hairsplitting distinctions between "Raca" and "You fool"? And could either be meaningfully spit out without anger? Jesus is simply multiplying examples to drive the lesson home. He is a preacher who makes his point and then makes his hearers feel its weight. He confronts his audience: You who think yourselves far removed, morally speaking, from murderers—have you not hated? Have you never wished someone were dead? Have you not frequently stooped to the use of contempt, even to character assassination? All such vilifying anger lies at the root of murder, and makes a thoughtful man conscious that he differs not a whit, morally speaking, from the actual murderer.

Similarly, it is doubtful that the three punishments—judgment, the Sanhedrin, and the fire of hell—are meant to be taken as a gradation. In the Old Testament theocracy, God himself stood behind the legal system of the state. Judgment, though civil, was also divine. Here, Jesus moves through the accepted system to the ultimate punishment to make it clear that the judgment to be feared is indeed divine, for it is based on God's assessment of the heart and can end in the fire of hell.

These verses make one great point. The Old Testament law forbidding murder must not be thought adequately satisfied when no blood has been shed. Rather, the law points toward a more fundamental problem, man's vilifying anger. Jesus by his own authority insists that the judgment thought to be reserved for the actual murderer in reality hangs over the wrathful, the spiteful, the contemptuous. What man then stands uncondemmed?

Someone may well ask, "But didn't Jesus himself get very angry sometimes?" Yes, that is true. He was certainly upset with the merchandising practiced in the temple precincts (Matt. 21:12ff. and parallels). Mark

records Jesus' anger with those who for legalistic and hypocritical reasons tried to find something wrong with the healings he performed on
the Sabbath (Mark 3:1ff.). And on one occasion Jesus addressed the
Pharisees and teachers of the law, "You blind fools!" (Matt. 23:17). Is
Jesus guilty of serious inconsistency?

Indeed there is a place for burning with anger at sin and injustice.
Our problem is that we burn with indignation and anger, not at sin and
injustice, but at offense to ourselves. In none of the cases in which Jesus
became angry was his personal ego wrapped up in the issue. More telling yet, when he was unjustly arrested, unfairly tried, illegally beaten,
contemptuously spit upon, crucified, mocked, when in fact he had every
reason for his ego to be involved, then, as Peter says, "he did not retaliate; when he suffered, he made no threats" (I Peter 2:23). From his
parched lips came forth rather those gracious words, "Father, forgive
them, for they do not know what they are doing" (Luke 23:34).

Let us admit it—by and large we are quick to be angry when we are
personally affronted and offended, and slow to be angry when sin and injustice multiply in other areas. In these cases we are more prone to phi-
losophize. In fact, the problem is even more complicated than that.
Sometimes we get involved in a legitimate issue and discern, perhaps
with accuracy, the right and the wrong of the matter. However, in push-
ing the right side, our own egos get so bound up with the issue that in
our view opponents are not only in the wrong but attacking us. When
we react with anger, we may deceive ourselves into thinking we are defending the truth and the right, when deep down we are more concerned
with defending ourselves.

In the Sermon on the Mount, despite the absolute cast in which anger
is forbidden, Jesus forbids not all anger but the anger which arises out of
personal relationships. This is obvious not only because of Jesus' teaching
and conduct elsewhere, and because the anger in question is that which
lies at the heart of murder, but also because of the two examples which
Jesus provides to give his point a cutting edge (5:23-26).

The first (5:23f.) concerns the person who comes to perform his religious duty (in this case the offering of a sacrifice at the temple altar)
but who has offended his brother. Jesus insists it is far more important
that he be reconciled to his brother than that he discharge his religious
duty; for the latter becomes pretense and sham if the worshiper has be-
haved so poorly that his brother has something against him. It is more
important to be cleared of offense before all men than to show up for
Sunday morning worship at the regular hour. Forget the worship service
and be reconciled to your brother; and only then worship God. Men love
to substitute ceremony for integrity, purity and love; but Jesus will have
none of it.

The second example (5:25f.) again picks up legal metaphor. In Jesus' day as in recent centuries, a person who defaulted in his debts could be thrown into a debtors' prison until the amount owed was paid. Of course, while he was there he couldn't earn anything, and therefore could scarcely be expected to pay off the debt and effect his own release; but his friends and loved ones who were eager to get him out might well put forth sustained and sacrificial efforts to provide the cash.

It would be making the metaphor run on all fours to deduce that Jesus is teaching that the heavenly court will condemn guilty people to "prison" (hell?) only until they've paid their debts. The debts in question are personal offenses; how then shall they be paid? And shall others pay the debt for the inmate? Rather, what Jesus is stressing is the urgency of personal reconciliation. Judgment is looming, and justice will be done: therefore keep clear of malice and offense toward others, for even the one "who is angry with his brother will be subject to judgment" (5:22). So we see that in both of these cases, it is *personal animosity* which is condemned.

Adultery and purity, 5:27-30

Jesus' contemporaries had also heard that it was said, "Do not commit adultery." This, of course, is a reference to the seventh of the ten commandments (Exod. 20:14).

Our society has moved a long way from this explicit prohibition. Many modern thinkers would affirm the legitimacy of adultery—if there is love. Even Christianity itself is invoked to sanctify this viewpoint. After all, it is argued, isn't love what the gospel is all about? In fact, as we shall see, such a philosophy distorts the biblical perspective of both love and marriage.

> In religion
> What damned error but some sober brow
> Will bless it and approve it with a text,
> Hiding the grossness with fair ornament.
> *Merchant of Venice*

As our society moves away from the seventh commandment in one direction, Jesus moves in another. He is not content with merely a formal adherence to it, nor is he simply interpreting it on the side of stringency. Rather, on his own authority he is underscoring the purity to which such a law points: "I tell you that anyone who looks at a woman lustfully has already committed adultery with her in his heart" (5:28). In effect, by labeling lust adultery, Jesus has deepened the seventh commandment in terms of the tenth, the prohibition of covetous-ness.

This is not a prohibition of the normal attraction which exists between men and women, but of the deep-seated lust which consumes and dev-ours, which in imagination attacks and rapes, which mentally contem-plates and commits adultery. If our society is easing off on the prohibition of adultery, how much more does it cater to our sexual lust? Our advertisements sell by sexual titillation; our bookstores fill their racks with both the salacious and the perverted. The vast majority of pop songs focus on man/woman relations, usually in terms of satisfying sex, physical desire, infidelity, and the like. Into this society Jesus speaks his piercing word: "Anyone who looks at a woman lustfully has already committed adultery with her in his heart." I write this line with shame: Which one of us in not guilty of adultery? Honesty before God in these matters may bring us the poverty of spirit which our triumphs never will, and prompt us to cry with the hymn writer,

> One thing I of the Lord desire—
> For all my way has darksome been—
> Be it by earthquake, wind or fire,
> Lord, make me clean. Lord, make me clean!
> *Walter Chalmers Smith (1824–1908)*

What we require is the attitude described by Jesus in 5:29f.: "If your right eye causes you to sin, gouge it out and throw it away. It is better for you to lose one part of your body than for your whole body to be thrown into hell. And if your right hand causes you to sin, cut it off and throw it away. It is better for you to lose one part of your body than for your whole body to go into hell." The eye is chosen because it has looked and lusted; the hand is chosen, probably because adultery, even mental adultery, is a kind of theft.

Some have taken this language literally. Origen (c. 195-254) castrated himself so that he would not be tempted. But that, I think, quite misses Jesus' point, and the absolute cast of Jesus' preaching noticed earlier; for if I gouged out my right eye because it had looked and lusted, would not my left do as well? And if I blinded myself, might I not lust anyway, and mentally gaze at forbidden things?

What then does Jesus mean? Just this: we are to deal drastically with sin. We must not pamper it, flirt with it, enjoy nibbling a little of it around the edges. We are to hate it, crush it, dig it out. "Put to death, therefore, whatever belongs to your earthly nature: sexual immorality, impurity, lust, evil desires and greed, which is idolatry" (Col. 3:5). Paul adds, "Because of these, the wrath of God is coming" (Col. 3:6)—just as

Jesus in Matthew 5:29f. threatens with hell all those who will not deal drastically with sin.

Our generation treats sin lightly. Sin in our society is better thought of as aberration, or as illness. It is to be treated, not condemned and repented of; and it must not be suppressed for fear of psychological damage. I am painfully aware how sin ensnares and entangles and produces pathetic victims; but the victims are not passive victims. In Jesus' teaching, sin leads to hell. And that is the ultimate reason why sin must be taken seriously.

Extrapolation
Divorce and remarriage, 5:31f.

The discussion of adultery and purity leads naturally to the question of divorce. The Jews of Jesus' day had heard it said that the man who wants to divorce his wife must give her a certificate of divorce. Actually, they were hearing something not quite true. The Old Testament passage to which appeal was made was Deuteronomy 24:1-4. The trust of that passage is this: If a man finds some uncleanness in his wife and divorces her, giving her a certificate of divorce, and she then marries someone else who in time also divorces her, then her first husband cannot remarry her.

By Jesus' day, this main principle was overlooked in favor of concentrating attention on the "uncleanness" which would make legitimate the first divorce. The particular expression for "uncleanness" is used only one other time in the Old Testament, where it refers to human defecation. What the sexual uncleanness is in Deuteronomy 24:1 is not clear; in any case it is, even in the Mosaic perspective, an exceptional thing. By Jesus' day, however, some even taught that it could be some imperfection in the wife as trivial as serving her husband food accidentally burned.

But Jesus will allow no sophistry. Here, as in Matthew 19:3ff., he goes back to first principles. In the beginning God made one man and one woman, and they were joined together. Initially, all divorce was inconceivable; when God made men and women, no allowance was made for it. The Creator said, "For this reason a man will leave his father and mother and be united to his wife, and the two will become one flesh." Jesus adds, "So they are no longer two, but one. Therefore what God has joined together, let man not separate" (Matt. 19:5f.). God in fact hates divorce (Mal. 2:16). Within this framework, therefore, it is obvious that if Moses permitted divorce for some gross uncleanness, it was an exception which found its *raison d'être* in man's hard, sinful heart.

In Matthew 5:31f., Jesus tightens up on the misconceptions, and shows the direction in which the Old Testament points. Anyone who divorces his wife is at fault, because he is causing her to commit adultery if she marries someone else, since the first link is not really broken. It follows therefore that the man who marries a divorcée is likewise committing adultery; before God he is in fact marrying another man's wife (5:32). The only exception which Jesus will allow is "fornication." Different Christians have said this word refers to all sorts of specific sins; but as far as I can see it is an inclusive term which refers to all sexual irregularity. For a married couple, it involves sexual marital unfaithfulness. Even in that case, a man is not commanded to divorce his wife, but permitted to, by way of concession. The same exceptive clause appears also in Matthew 19, and refers both to divorce and remarriage.

This is not all the Bible has to say on the subject, and a great deal of care must be taken in putting it all together. But this is at the heart of it, and our generation needs to be confronted with these demands. It used to be that divorce was a problem rarely found in evangelical circles. To our shame, that is no longer the case. Our society, including many professing Christians, has rejected biblical conceptions of both love and marriage. Love has become a mixture of physical desire and vague sentimentality; marriage has become a provisional sexual union to be terminated when this pathetic, pygmy love dissolves.

How different is the biblical perspective! In God's Word, marriage and love are for the tough-minded. Marriage is commitment; and, far from backing out when the going gets rough, marriage partners are to sort out their difficulties in the light of Scripture. They are to hang in there, improving their relationship, working away at it, precisely because they have vowed before God and man to live together and love each other for better, for worse, for richer, for poorer, in sickness as in health, until death separates them. Love is the determined commitment to seek the other's good, to cherish, shelter, nurture, edify, and show patience with one's partner. And this commitment, worked out because of deep-rooted obedience to God, brings with it the emotional and sentimental aspects of love as well.

Jesus presupposes this high view of marriage when, with one concessive exception, he flatly prohibits divorce. And it is this high view of marriage which likewise underlies Jesus' trenchant remarks on lust (5:27-30), and gives this block of material (5:27-32) its unity. Marriage is not dirty, sex is not filthy. Both are wonderful gifts from the Creator; but they are prostituted by lust, and demeaned by divorce. The Law and the Prophets, by Jesus' own authority, point to the necessity of absolute purity and must not be trivialized by sophistries which seek to escape that purity.

Oaths and truthfulness, 5:33-37

In the third block of material, Jesus deals with the question of truthfulness. The people had heard that it was said long ago, "Do not break your oath, but keep the oaths you have made to the Lord" (5:33). This is not a direct quotation from the Old Testament, but an allusion to such passages as Exodus 20:7, Leviticus 19:12, Numbers 30:2, and Deuteronomy 23:21-24. But Jesus now says, "Do not swear at all" (5:34).

Some people think this prohibits them from taking oaths in a courtroom, or from taking an oath of allegiance. Their desire to obey God's Word is admirable; but I submit they have really not understood it. As usual, Jesus is preaching in antithetical fashion; and it is important to discover just what he is saying before we take his statement with such insensitive absoluteness.

It needs to be noticed, first, that the Old Testament does permit men to take oaths, even oaths in God's name. "You shall fear the Lord your God. Him you will serve, to him you will cleave, and you will swear by his name" (Deut. 10:20). Even in the New Testament, Paul, for example, regularly swears by God's name. In particular, he calls God as his witness (Rom. 1:9; II Cor. 1:23; I Thess. 2:5, 10; cf. Phil. 1:8). Therefore if Paul knew of this teaching of Jesus, he certainly did not take it absolutely. God himself swears: he swears not to send another universal flood (Gen. 9:9-11), he swears to send a redeemer (Luke 1:68, 73), to raise his Son from the dead (Ps. 16:10; Acts 2:27-31), and much more.

Now all of this swearing, these oaths, are designed to encourage truthfulness, or to make truthfulness the more solemn and sure. Sometimes this is even spelled out for us. For example, in one case we read, "Because God wanted to make the unchanging nature of his purpose very clear to the heirs of what was promised, he confirmed it with an oath" (Heb. 6:17). For the same reason, the Mosaic code forbade only false or irreverent oaths, which must be regarded as profaning God's name.

Unfortunately, however, by Jesus' time the Jews had built up an entire legalistic system around the Old Testament teaching. In the Jewish code of law called the *Mishnah*, there is one whole tractate given over to the question of oaths, including detailed consideration of when they're binding and when they're not. For example, one rabbi says that if you swear *by* Jerusalem you are not bound by your vow; but if you swear *toward* Jerusalem, then you are bound by your vow. The swearing of oaths thus degenerates into terrible rules which let you know when you can get away with lying and deception, and when you can't. These oaths no longer foster truthfulness, but weaken the cause of truth and promote deceit. Swearing evasively becomes justification for lying.

Jesus will not allow such casuistry among his followers. If men will play such games with oaths, Jesus will simply abolish oaths. He is interested in truthfulness, its constancy and absoluteness.

Jesus gives examples. Men are not to swear by the heaven or by the earth, for they are God's throne and his footstool respectively. They must not swear toward Jerusalem (if we translate the preposition literally) for it is the city of God, the great King. They must not even swear by their head (compare I Sam. 1:26; Ps. 15:4), for they cannot so much as change the color of a single hair: that is, they are swearing by something over which God alone has ultimate sway. In other words, Jesus relates every oath to God; to swear by anything is to swear by God, for God in some way stands behind everything. Therefore no oath is trivial, no oath is justifiable evasion; all oaths are solemn pledges to speak the truth. Jesus enlarges on this point elsewhere:

> Woe to you, blind guides! You say, "If anyone swears by the temple, it means nothing; but if anyone swears by the gold of the temple, he is bound by his oath." You blind fools! Which is greater: the gold, or the temple that makes the gold sacred? You also say, "If anyone swears by the altar, it means nothing; but if anyone swears by the gift on it, he is bound by his oath." You blind men! Which is greater: the gift, or the altar that makes the gift sacred? Therefore, he who swears by the altar swears by it and by everything on it. And he who swears by the temple swears by it and by the one who dwells in it. And he who swears by heaven swears by God's throne and by the one who sits on it (Matt. 23:16-22).

The real question here is truthfulness. For the follower of Jesus, it is best simply to say "Yes" and mean yes, to say "No" and mean no. In the context of Jesus' day, anything beyond this comes from the evil one (5:37), who is well-named the father of lies (John 8:44). Jesus' teaching in this matter of truthfulness left a big impression on the early church, for in what is probably the first epistle in the New Testament to have been written, the epistle of James, the same point is emphasized (James 5:12).

Christians claim to have the truth, and to follow him who is the Truth (John 14:6). In our conversations, therefore, truth must be our watchword. How many of us stoop to telling stories with a reprehensible slant, either to make our point more emphatically or to present ourselves in a more glamorous light than the raw facts will allow? How many of us say we will do things and instead renege on these responsibilities because it is personally inconvenient to go through with them? You who with me are teachers and preachers—how often do we fudge the evidence to make a point, or dogmatize in areas where we know nothing, in the hope that dogma will mask our ignorance? I am not speaking of the honest mistake, but of deceit. Our Lord insists that the Old Testament Scriptures point toward truthfulness; and all who submit to his authority cannot be too careful to speak only truth.

Personal abuse and personal self-sarifice, 5:38-42

The Jewish people had heard that it was said, "An eye for an eye, and a tooth for a tooth." This famous law is found in Exodus 21, Leviticus 24, and Deuteronomy 19. Two things must be remembered about this law. First, however prescriptive it might have been, it was also restrictive; and therefore it was an excellent tool for eliminating blood feuds and inter-tribal warfare. Suppose someone cuts off my brother's hand, and I go and knock off the assailant's head. Immediately the initial violence has been escalated, and the assailant's family may feel honor-bound to butcher both me and my family. Where then will it end? But if, instead, the initial act of violence is met with reprisal in precisely the same kind and degree, an eye for an eye and a tooth for a tooth, that is the end of the matter. Second, the law was given to the Jewish people *qua* nation. The law was not designed to be discharged by individuals swept up in personal vendettas, but by the judiciary.

By Jesus' day, however, both of these fundamentals were frequently overlooked. It became all too easy to see the law as prescriptive, and only marginally restrictive. The question then became, How far may my personal retaliation extend, without breaking the law? Worse, the law was thus being dragged into the personal arena, where it could scarcely foster even rough justice, but only bitterness, vengeance, malice, hatred.

Jesus responds with sweeping authority: "But I tell you, Do not resist an evil person" (5:39). How is this statement to be taken? Tolstoy's view that there should be no soldiers, policemen, or magistrates because they resist evil people became famous. But note carefully what Tolstoy is doing: he is extending Jesus' statement to mean that no one may resist an evil person *who is attacking a third party*. For example, twice in my life I have stumbled into a scene in which my physical presence prevented violence. Both occurred late at night in the slums of Toronto. In one, a fellow was attacking a girl; he ran off as I approached. In the other, a drunk was using a bottle to menace a couple as they cowered in a corner. I put myself between the drunk and the couple, whom I urged to leave with appropriate alacrity. Naturally, the drunk turned on me; but as it happened, he never did try to thrust his bottle in my face, and so I was spared the necessity of having to relieve him of it. Nevertheless, it can scarcely be denied that I was guilty of resisting an evil person. Does Jesus' injunction condemn me for my action?

Not many would answer in the affirmative. However, many Christians would be prepared to argue, on the basis of what Jesus here says, that no *Christian* should ever resist evil directed at *him,* and therefore in principle no *Christian* should ever join a police force or an army. They acknowledge that God has given the power of the sword to the *state* (cf. Rom. 13:1-7), but conclude that no Christian should ever be found in any force or position of civil authority which would require him to resist evil people. These committed pacifists feel that any other alternative dilutes what Jesus teaches in the Sermon on the Mount.*

This problem is not an easy one, and what I write is not likely to resolve it. However, it is necessary to make due allowance for both the background in which Jesus was preaching, and the antithetical form of his utterances, so typical of him. All interpretations of the text do this at some point or another. For example, Jesus says in 5:42, "Give to the one who asks you." In Cambridge, England, where I first presented this material in lecture form, a large number of beggars prey on the student population, with constant and frenquently belligerent demands for handouts. Some of these men are in dire need, and it is a shame there is still no adequate center for them. But many are just using the students. They get to know the softhearted ones, and literally prey on them. Several times when I have been approached for money for food or for shelter, I have offered a meal, offered my time to try to find lodging, and the like; but, when I would not simply give money, my offers were spurned and I was roundly cursed for my pains. The money in question was allegedly to buy food or to provide shelter; but in too many cases it was spent on drink.

Is it the Christian's responsibility to shell out to the professional beggar, or to pay for the drug that is ruining another man? By saying, "Give to the one who asks you," does Jesus mean there are no circumstances where that injunction may not apply? I know a Cambridge research student whose tender conscience led him to an affirmative answer to that question, and who went bankrupt as a result, quite literally doing without food himself while he supplied half a dozen men with the alcohol they would have been better off without. Eventually he was helped to see that his actions, though well motivated, were helping neither the men nor himself, and were honoring neither Jesus nor his teaching.

Thus, no matter how much we wish to follow Jesus seriously, we discover, sooner or later, that seriously following Jesus entails hard thinking about what he said and what he did not say. We may not come to perfect unanimity on all points; but we must agree that absolutizing any text, without due respect for the context and flow of the argument, as

---

*Perhaps the best recent defense of this position is by J. H. Yoder in his book, *The Politics of Jesus* (Eerdmans).

well as for other things Jesus says elsewhere, is bound to lead to distortion and misrepresentation of what Jesus means.

As I understand these verses, I do not think that Jesus has policemen and soldiers in view. Explicit New Testament teaching concerning such occupations has more to do with integrity, contentment with wages, and the like.*

Instead Jesus is speaking in Matthew 5:38-42 of *personal* abuse and *personal* self-sacrifice, using the misunderstanding of Old Testament law as his starting point. The four examples he gives bear this out.

The first concerns a sharp backhand slap to the cheek, a gross insult. The follower of Jesus is to be prepared to take another one rather than retaliate. There are famous stories of the transformed characters of people like Billy Bray, the pugilist, or of Tom Skinner, leader of the Harlem Lords, when they were converted. Once tough, hostile and belligerent, they meekly accepted insults and blows (and thereby deeply impressed some of their assailants). This attitude is especially important, of course, when the violence and abuse have come about because of some stand for righteousness (cf. 5:10-12); but the text need not be restricted to that.

The second example concerns a lawsuit in which a man is likely to lose his "tunic," a long garment which corresponds to a modern dress or suit of clothes. The follower of Jesus will throw in the outer coat as well, even though this latter garment was recognized by Jewish law to be an inalienable possession (Exod. 22:26f.). It is unlikely, of course, that a lawsuit would be fought over a suit of clothes. But at stake here is a principle: even those things which we regard as our rights by law we must be prepared to abandon. In another context, Paul enlarges on this principle when he insists that followers of Jesus will prefer to be wronged rather than to enter litigation with another follower of Jesus (I Cor. 6:7f.).

The third example probably refers to the Roman practice of commandeering civilians. "If someone forces you to go one mile, go with him two miles" (5:41). An ordinary Roman soldier could legally commandeer a civilian to help him, for example, to carry his luggage for a prescribed distance. Jesus' followers are not to feel hard done by and irritable in such cases, as if personally insulted, but are to double the distance and accept the imposition cheerfully.

Jesus' last example demands giving and lending that is cheerful and willing. The issue is not the wisdom or foolishness of lending money to

---

*For those who want to read a Christian perspective on violence and on state authority, written at a popular level and with emphases with which I sympathize, see chapter five of Os Guinness, *The Dust of Death* (InterVarsity Press).

everyone who comes along (for which see Prov. 11:15; 17:18; 22:26), just as Cambridge beggars are not the issue. The burden of the passage is this: Christ will not tolerate a mercenary, tight-fisted, penny-pinching attitude which is the financial counterpart to a legalistic understanding of "An eye for an eye, and a tooth for a tooth." "Give to the one who asks you, and do not turn away from the one who wants to borrow from you" (5:42). Don't be asking yourself all the time, "What's in it for me? What can I get out of it?"

The legalistic mentality which dwells on retaliation and so-called fairness makes much of one's rights. What Jesus is saying in these verses, more than anything else, is that his followers have no rights. They do not have the right to retaliate and wreck their vengeance (5:39), they do not have the right to their possessions (5:40), nor to their time and money (5:41f.). Even their legal rights may sometimes be abandoned (5:40). Hence, it would completely miss the point to interpret 5:41, for example, to mean that the follower of Christ will be prepared to go two miles, but not one inch further! Personal self-sacrifice displaces personal retaliation; for this is the way the Savior himself went, the way of the cross. And the way of the cross, not notions of "right and wrong," is the Christian's principle of conduct.

Hatred and love, 5:43-47

Consideration of personal abuse and of the response of self-sacrifice leads naturally to the broader question of hatred and love. The people had heard that it was said, "Love your neighbor and hate your enemy" (5:43). Again, they were hearing falsely. The Old Testament Scriptures say, "Love your neighbor" (Lev. 19:18), but nowhere "Hate your enemy." But some Jews took the word "neighbor" to be exclusive: we are to love *only* our neighbors, they thought, and therefore we are to hate our enemies.

This was actually taught in some circles. In the monastic community which lived by the Dead Sea, a common dictum was, "Love the brothers; hate the outsider." The problem of identifying the "neighbor" was a live issue in Jesus' day. It was this very question which prompted Jesus to tell the parable of the Good Samaritan (Luke 10:29ff.), in which Jesus points out that one's neighbor is anyone he is in a position to help. "Love your enemies," Jesus says, "and pray for those who persecute you" (5:44). The particular enemies on whom Jesus focuses attention are the persecutors, presumably those who persecute his followers because of righteousness, because of Jesus himself (5:10-12). To love them and to pray for them is an important part of being a son of the heavenly Father. After all, God "causes his sun to rise on the evil and the good, and sends rain on the righteous and the unrighteous" (5:45). God loved rebellious sinners so much he sent his Son (John 3:16; Rom. 5:8); and, if we are his sons, we will have his character. To be persecuted because of righteousness is to align oneself with the prophets (5:12); but to bless and pray for those who persecute us is to align oneself with the character of God.

Nowhere is this sublime attitude more explicit than in Jesus himself, who, while suffering the unjust agony of the cross, cried, "Father, forgive them, for they do not know what they are doing" (Luke 23:34). In the light of such a standard, it will not do merely to love one's friends and let it go at that. "If you love those who love you, what reward will you get? Are not even the tax collectors doing that?"

Tax collectors may have a bad name today; but it is nothing like the reputation they earned in first-century Palestine. The Roman Empire used a tax-farming system. The government would specify the amount to be collected from a certain area, and appoint a man to gather it. This man would in turn appoint men under him, who would appoint others under them. Each appointee had to obtain his quota, and whatever else he got he could keep. The potential for bribery and corruption all the way up the tax farming ladder was enormous, and every avenue was assiduously exploited. Naturally, the Jewish tax collectors were loathed, and doubly loathed among the Jews because they came into contact with the Gentiles, the Roman overlords, and thus became ceremonially unclean. But even these low, traitorous, disgusting people enjoyed friends—other tax collectors, for a start! So how is a disciple of Jesus in any way superior to the despised tax collector if he only loves his friends?

"And if you greet only your brothers, what are you doing more than others? Do not even pagans do that?" (5:47). A greeting can say a great deal, especially if it brings a wish of welfare and well-being. If certain people are carefully ignored, and only those close to us receive our sincere good wishes, how do we differ from pagans? In other words, the follower of Jesus must not stoop to the low standards of his society. He is, rather, to pattern himself after his heavenly Father. The disciple of Jesus will stand out in the world because of the divine quality of his love. Indeed, elsewhere Jesus even elevates love among Christians to the characteristic or mark that indicates they belong to him (John 13:34f.). Thus it is that Jesus makes clear the real direction toward which the Old Testament law points. It points to a higher standard than legalism and casuistry can ever admit.

CONCLUSION: THE DEMAND FOR PERFECTION
Matthew 5:48

As we have seen, to love one's enemies is characteristic of God (5:45). But love is not the only characteristic of God which Jesus expects his followers to emulate. As the passage continues, it becomes painfully obvious that Jesus is setting out a breathtaking description of morality which makes God himself the standard of all of it. "Be perfect, therefore, as your heavenly Father is perfect" (5:48).

We are to be holy, for the Lord our God is holy (Lev. 19:2); loving, because God is love (I John 4:7ff.); perfect, as our heavenly Father is perfect (Matt. 5:48).

There are two final points to observe about this section of the Sermon on the Mount. First, Jesus' authority is one of the most dominant features in this chapter. The Law and the Prophets point toward him, but he himself determines their meaning, fulfillment, and continuity, with an authority nothing less than divine. It is important to remember that the Old Testament Scriptures have no intrinsic status apart from God—whatever authority they possess is derived. But because the derivation is *from God,* it takes nothing less than divine authority to interpret it and define it in this way; implicitly, therefore, Jesus is claiming such authority for himself.

Second, that toward which the Law and the Prophets have pointed has come in the person of Jesus and in the kingdom (the saving reign) which he introduces. Jesus authoritatively makes plain the demands of the kingdom and how they stand in relation to the Old Testament Scriptures. The common demand is holiness, perfection; all the Old Testament laws are rightly understood only when interpreted in the light of this overwhelming concern. The emphasis on transparent purity and unaffected holiness, on imitating the Father's perfection, utterly precludes all religious hypocrisy, all spiritual sham, all paraded righteousness, all ostentatiously performed religious duties. But this deduction Jesus himself makes explicit in Matthew 6.

RELIGIOUS HYPOCRISY:

Its Description and Overthrow

THE PRINCIPLE
Matthew 6:1

We human beings are a strange lot. We hear high moral injunctions and glimpse just a little the genuine beauty of perfect holiness, and then prostitute the vision by dreaming about the way others would hold us in high esteem if we were like that. The demand for genuine perfection loses itself in the lesser goal of external piety; the goal of pleasing the Father is traded for its pygmy cousin, the goal of pleasing men. It almost seems as if the greater the demand for holiness, the greater the opportunity for hypocrisy. This is why I suspect that the danger is potentially most serious among religious leaders.

Jesus, having demanded of his followers nothing less than perfection (5:48), is fully aware of the human heart's propensity for self-deception, and issues a strong warning. "Be careful not to do your 'acts of righteousness' before men, to be seen by them. If you do, you will have no reward from your Father in heaven" (6:1). Be perfect (5:48), but be careful (6:1). The question of whose approval we are seeking is thus raised in another form. Just as the beatitudes ask me if it is God's blessing I want, or some other approval, so the demands of righteousness, as presented by Jesus, can never legitimately be confused with forms of external piety: the righteousness in question pleases the Father and is rewarded by him.

The King James Version begins chapter 6 with the words, "Take heed that ye do not your alms before men, to be seen of them. . . ." In other words, it introduces the question of alms in verse 1 instead of verse 2. But the oldest and best manuscripts preserve the reading of the New International Version. Jesus reserves verse 1 for the general principle: All "acts of righteousness" must be preserved from the ostentation of showmanship and from the degradation of the chase for human approval. Then in verses 2-18, he focuses on the three fundamental acts of Jewish piety, i.e., almsgiving (6:2-4), prayer (6:5-15), and fasting (6:16-18). He selects these three to represent all other "acts of righteousness," treating each in the same way. First, he offers a description and a denunciation of that particular form of ostentatious piety typical of the more degenerate forms of Pharisaism, both ancient and modern. Second, he gives an ironic affirmation of the limited results of such pseudo-piety: the actors receive their reward in full. The reward is understood to be the acclaim of the fickle crowd. And that is all the actors get. Third, he presents a contrasting description of true piety and its results. Let us trace this form in the three examples.

THE EXAMPLES
Matthew 6:2-18

Alms, 6:2-4

The biblical revelation has always held to the importance of almsgiving, of giving to needy people (see Deut. 15:11; Ps. 41:1; Prov. 19:17). But much of our giving is less concerned with meeting needs and pleasing God than with earning a reputation for generosity and piety.

"So when you give to the needy, do not announce it with trumpets, as the hypocrites do in the synagogues and on the streets, to be honored by men" (6:2). The trumpets may be metaphorical; philanthropy is not to be accompanied by the repulsive sound of the philanthropist blowing his own horn. But the trumpets may be literal, the trumpets of the Jerusalem temple calling the citizens together to contribute to some particularly urgent need. The opportunity for ostentation under such circumstances is quite unmatched—the trumpets sound, and I quickly close my shop and hasten down the street. Everyone knows where I'm going, and the speed at which I'm moving not only draws attention to my direction but attests to my zeal.

However, Jesus says that people who give in such a fashion, whether in the street or in the synagogue, whether in churches or toward charities, whether as a company public relations gimmick or as a personal effort at self-promotion—these people are hypocrites.

There are several different kinds of hypocrisy. In one kind, the hypocrite feigns goodness but is actually evil, like those who tried to "catch"

Jesus in things he said (Matt. 22:15ff.). Such hypocrites know they are being deceptive. In another kind of hypocrisy, the hypocrite is puffed up with his own importance and self-righteousness. Blind to his own faults, he may be genuinely unaware that he is hypocritical—even though he is very harsh toward other people and their sins. Jesus discusses such hypocrites in Matthew 7:1-5, as we shall see. We may at least comfort ourselves that onlookers readily detect this form of hypocrisy, even if the hypocrite himself remains oblivious to his own double standard.

But the kind of hypocrisy involved in Matthew 6:2 is more subtle than either of the other two. In this case, the hypocrite has talked himself into believing that at heart, he is conducting himself with the best interests of the needy in mind. He may thus be unaware of his own hypocrisy. Moreover, the needy themselves are not likely to complain; they will be touchingly grateful, and contribute to the giver's self-delusion. And all but the most discerning of onlookers will speak appreciatively of the philanthropist's deed, for all acknowledge that giving is good.

A hypocrite is basically an actor—consciously or unconsciously. In fact, the classical Greek word, here translated "hypocrite," originally meant actor. Hypocritical piety is not from the heart, it is not genuine; it is play-acting piety. This kind of philanthropy is still motivated by a form of egoism. In the secret recesses of their cherished ambitions, such hypocrites give in order "to be honored by men." And, says Jesus, "I tell you the truth, they have received their reward in full" (6:2b). They get what they're after; but that's all they get. The whole thing turns out to be a successful public relations stunt, and no more. There is no real "act of righteousness," no genuine piety—and no reward from God.

"But when you give to the needy, do not let your left hand know what your right hand is doing, so that your giving may be in secret" (6:3-4a). It is almost as if the Master is using an overwhelming metaphor to express adequately just how quiet and private our giving ought to be. Such privacy is not itself meritorious; but it ensures that our giving is not prompted, even in part, by a love for the praise of peers. No one will know what we have given; and, if there is a danger that secret pride will be nurtured, we ourselves are scarcely to know what we've given: the left hand remains ignorant of what the right hand gives. No one will know about this giving in secret; no one, that is, but God.

Precisely because the Father alone knows, such secret giving is another way of assuring that we are performing a genuine "act of righteousness," one that is pleasing to him. He will detect that we have given because of real compassion for the needy and out of a transparent desire to please him. In this sense, we will be like the Corinthians who first gave *themselves* to the Lord, and then gave their money to the Lord's work (II Cor. 8:5).

So we are to give "secretly," both to protect ourselves from ostentatious pseudo-piety, and to ensure that we are acting righteously before the Lord. "Then," says Jesus, "your Father, who sees in secret, will reward you" (6:4). It is again made clear that the follower of Jesus is interested in the rewards and blessings of God, and not in the transient approval of men. And, as we understand from the text, Jesus' disciple is not giving secretly *in order to* win some heavenly reward; rather he is giving secretly to avoid the glamor of honor from men, to please his heavenly Father, and to meet real need. The *result* is spiritual reward.

Clearly, Jesus is not opposed to giving; indeed, he presupposes that his followers will give. But his followers, whose goal is perfection, must not delude themselves into thinking that all giving pleases him, or that giving *per se* is an "act of righteousness." The human heart is too crafty to allow so simple a suggestion to stand.

Prayer, 6:5-8

"When you pray, do not be like the hypocrites, for they love to pray in the synagogues and on the street corners to be seen by men. I tell you the truth, they have received their reward in full" (6:5). Play-acting almsgiving now gives way to play-acting praying. As Jesus was not opposed to almsgiving, so is he not opposed to prayer. He presupposes that his followers *will* pray: "*When* you pray. . . ." What he categorically rejects is the attitude found in these who "love to pray . . . to be seen by men."

In synagogue services public prayer was customarily led by a male member of the congregation who stood in front of the ark of the law and discharged this responsibility. A man could easily succumb to the temptation of praying up to the audience/congregation. The acceptable clichés, the appropriate sentiments, the sonorous tones, the well-pitched fervency, all become tools to win approval, and perhaps to compete with the chap who led in prayer last week.

Moreover, at times of public fasts, and perhaps at the time of the daily afternoon temple sacrifice, the trumpets would blow as a sign that prayer should be offered. Right where he was, in the street, a man would turn and face the temple to offer his prayer. This opportunity for a little ostentatious piety was really quite gratifying.

I don't think we should be too hard on the Jews of Jesus' day before examining ourselves thoroughly. I am painfully aware of my own capacity for self-delusion and deceit; and I suspect I am not an isolated case. The believer requested to pray in a Baptist service, the reader asked to participate in an Anglican evensong, the brother asked to preach in a Brethren meeting, the student asked to read the Scripture in Pres-

byterian worship, and the minister in any of them, have all been sorely
tempted in this area. And all receive the same reward, the human praise
they desire. But that is their full reward; there is no other, and certainly
no answered prayer from the Lord himself.

What, then, is to characterize our prayers? Jesus mentions two things.
First: "When you pray, go into your room, close the door and pray to
your Father, who is unseen. Then your Father, who sees what is done in
secret, will reward you" (6:6). Again, I doubt if Jesus is trying to pro-
hibit all public prayer. If so, the early church didn't understand him, if
we may judge by the examples of public praying in the Book of Acts
(1:24; 3:1; 4:24ff.; etc.). We will comprehend Jesus' point better if we
each ask ourselves these questions: Do I pray more frequently and more
fervently when alone with God than I do in public? Do I love the secret
place of prayer? Is my public praying simply the overflow of my private
praying? If the answers are not enthusiastic affirmatives, we fail the test
and fall under Jesus' condemnation. We are hypocrites.

Could it be that the prime reason we do not see more prayers answered is because we are less concerned with bringing our requests to
God than with showing off before men? There is a frequently repeated
story of a minister in New England who described an elaborate and
polished prayer offered in a fashionable Boston church as "the most
eloquent prayer ever offered to a Boston audience." Just so. What do I
think about when I am praying in public? Am I so busy scrambling to
find expressions pleasing to my fellow worshipers that I am not really
concentrating my attention on God, and scarcely aware of his presence,
even though he is the One to whom my prayers are nominally
addressed? Jesus insists that the best way to overcome such evils is to
spend time in secret prayer. "Then your Father, who sees what is done
in secret, will reward you."

Jesus mentions a second thing which must characterize our praying:
"And when you pray, do not keep on babbling like pagans, for they
think they will be heard because of their many words. Do not be like
them, for your Father knows what you need before you ask him" (6:7f.).
Some pagans thought that if they named all their gods, and addressed
their petitions to each of them, and then repeated themselves a few
times, they would have a better chance of receiving an answer. Jesus
tells his contemporary Jewish hearers that much of their praying is akin
to this babbling found among pagans; and I am certain that if he were
addressing us directly today he would tell us the same thing. Prayer
should not consist of heaped-up phrases, idle repetitions, and the ridiculous assumption that the probability of an answer is in proportion to the
total number of words in the prayer. "Do not be rash with your mouth or
impulsive in thought to bring up anything before God. For God is in

heaven and you are on the earth: therefore let your words be few"
(Eccles. 5:2). It is shameful to think we can wrest favors from God by
the sheer volume of prayer, mechanically intoned.

In one church where I ministered, it was a regular custom in our mid-
week prayer meeting for the men and boys to go off and pray in one
area of the building and the women and girls in another. Some churches,
of course, have much smaller breakdowns. There are advantages to
smaller groups—for a start, more people can participate. But there are
also disadvantages. There is a genuine need for times when the whole
church family prays together, partly to promote unity and partly so that
each group within the church learns of the spiritual concerns of the others. In any case, I had inherited this segregated situation and felt it was
only one option, not a necessary part of the ecclesiastical tradition. So
one night I gently suggested that we all meet to pray together, at least
for that week. After the meeting was over, one good man came to me
deeply troubled. He felt we had wasted time because "not as much praying could be done." It was true, of course, that not as many individuals
led in prayer out loud; but there was no reason why just as many as ever
could not have prayed. And in any case, *the sheer volume of words is
not the crucial factor,* scarcely even an important factor.

But isn't sustained praying important? What about the parable in
Luke 18:1-8, where Jesus tells a story with the explicit purpose of
teaching them that men "should always pray and not give up" (Luke
18:1)?

I think we have once more stumbled onto a pattern noticed already in
other connections. Jesus has a way of preaching in absolute categories
even when he is primarily addressing himself to fairly specific conditions. Unless this is taken into account, we may neglect or distort what
he says elsewhere on the same subject but under different conditions.

To put it another way: Jesus offers much of his teaching with certain
relationships in view. His teaching never smacks of systematic theology.
Such theology is no doubt a legitimate discipline; but if theology system-
atizes a particular teaching of Jesus too early in its study, it may be guilty
of minimizing other relevant teachings of Jesus. It may also negate the
implicit limitations imposed on a particular passage by the pattern of
relationships Jesus used in that instance.

In the particular example before us, if we absolutize Matthew 6:7f.,
the logical conclusion is that followers of Jesus must never pray at
length, and seldom if ever ask for anything since God knows their needs
anyway. If instead we absolutize Luke 18:1-8, we will reason that if we
are serious with God we will not only pray at length, but we may expect
the blessings we receive to be proportionate to our loquacity. However,
if we listen to *both* passages with a little more sensitivity, we discover

that Matthew 6:7f. is really not concerned with the length of prayers, but with the attitude of heart which thinks it is heard for its many words. Likewise, we find that Luke 18:1-8 is less concerned with mere length of prayers than with overcoming the quitting tendency among certain of Christ's followers. These Christians, finding themselves under pressure, are often in danger of throwing in the towel. But they must not give up.

The best example in this matter of praying is Jesus himself. Although he prayed much in public, he prayed far more in private; the evangelist Luke takes special pains to demonstrate this (see Luke 5:16; 6:12; 9:18, 28; 11:1; 22:41f.). Although he sometimes prayed with pithy brevity, he also gave himself to long, nighttime vigils. And he taught his followers to address God as their Father, assuring them at the same time that this heavenly Father not only knows the needs of his children before they ask him, yet also encourages those children to ask, in confidence and trust.

In sum: Jesus wants to teach us that praying, to be a genuine act of righteousness, must be without ostentation, directed to the Father and not to men, primarily private, and devoid of the delusion that God can be manipulated by empty garrulity.

How, then, should we pray? Jesus himself gives us a wonderful example, usually referred to as "The Lord's Prayer," but more appropriately designated "The Lord's Model Prayer," since it is less the prayer he prayed than the prayer he gave his disciples as a paradigm for their own praying.

Extrapolation
The Lord's Model Prayer, 6:9-15

It is ironic that the context which forbids meaningless repetition in prayer serves in Matthew's Gospel as the location of the Lord's model prayer; for no prayer has been repeated more than this, very often without understanding. As early as the second century, a document now referred to as the *Didache* prescribes that Christians should repeat this prayer three times a day. That is not necessarily bad, just as it is not necessarily bad to repeat it in unison in our church services. But we must never do so thoughtlessly, and we should remember that Jesus himself conceived of the prayer as a model: "This is how you should pray" (6:9a), he said, not, "This is *what* you should pray."

There are six petitions in this prayer. It is appropriate that the first three concern God directly: his name, his kingdom, his will. The Christian's primary concerns therefore are that God's name be hallowed, that his kingdom come, that his will be done on earth as it is in heaven.

Only then are the next three petitions introduced, and they have to do with man directly: our daily food, our sins ("our debts") and our temptations. It is encouraging that in this model prayer Jesus' thought embraces both our physical and our spiritual needs.

Before looking at these six petitions in a little more detail, we ought to focus attention on the opening invocation: "Our Father in heaven." Jesus did not teach us to pray, "*My* Father in heaven," but "*Our* Father in heaven." Christians are not to pray in splendid isolation, and not to construe spirituality in terms of the rugged individualism which stamps so much Western thought. The apostle John reflects a major New Testament theme when he says, in I John 5:1, "Everyone who believes that Jesus is the Christ is born of God, and everyone who loves the father [i.e. God] loves his child as well [i.e. other Christians.]" There is, no doubt, a place for praying as an individual to God; but the general pattern of our praying must be broader than that. Therefore, when I as one follower of Christ among many, address *our* Father, my concern is to embrace *our* daily bread, *our* sins, and *our* temptations—and not just *mine*.

Concerning the designation "Father," three things need to be said. First, although it is found in Jewish writings about the time of Christ, it is extremely rare. A well-known German scholar, Joachim Jeremias, has shown how exceptional and how stunning Jesus' use of this form of address must have been to his first followers. The Jews of this period preferred exalted titles for God, like "Sovereign Lord," "King of the Universe," and the like. Jesus called him Father (cf. Matt 11:25; 26:39, 42; Mark 14:36; Luke 23:34; John 11:41; 12:27; 17:1, 5, 11, 21, 24f.). "*Abba*," he said to God; and this is an Aramaic word used by children to address their father. It is not quite as familiar as "My Daddy," but more familiar than "My Father." It reminds me of the way French-speaking Canadian children frequently address their fathers: "Papa."

Of course, Jesus was the Son of God in a unique sense; God was uniquely his Father. Jesus' manner of addressing God forms part of a larger picture in which he claimed, in scores of different ways, to be uniquely one with God. But the remarkable thing about the model prayer before us is that Jesus is here teaching *his disciples* to address God in the same way.

This observation brings us to another major New Testament theme. It is common for New Testament writers to describe the process of becoming a disciple of Jesus in terms of becoming a child of God, a son of God. Those who repent of their sins and trust Jesus as the one who paid for their sins by dying in their behalf, those who vow allegiance and obedience to Jesus, those who confess, "Jesus is Lord!"—these are the same ones who are said to be born of God (John 3), sons of God by adoption (Rom. 8). Once headed for wrath (Eph. 2:3), now these people have been made alive before God. They relish the new relationship with God himself. Although their sonship is in some respects qualitatively different from Jesus' sonship, nevertheless they along with Christ will inherit the splendors of a new heaven and earth (Rom. 8: 15ff.). Even now, God has sent the Spirit of his Son into their hearts, the Spirit who calls out, "*Abba*, Father" (Gal. 4:6). Small wonder that Jesus, after his death and resurrection, could triumphantly instruct Mary, "Go to my brothers and tell them, 'I am returning to *my* Father and *your* Father, to *my* God and *your* God'" (John 20:17). By his ministry, death, and resurrection, Jesus brought about the means whereby men could come to God Almighty and say, meaningfully, "Our Father."

This, then, is the second thing that needs to be said about such a designation: The way in which God is seen as a Father in the Scripture is usually related, not to the general "Fatherhood of God" ("God is the Father, and all men are brothers"), but to the special relationship between God and followers of Jesus. It is true, of course, that all men everywhere are "God's children" (Acts 17:29) in the sense that God made them all and stands over them as Creator and Sustainer, and yet that is not the way New Testament writers most commonly use the "father-son" imagery with respect to God and men. For example, in I John 3:1 John distinguishes between "children of God" and "the world." Writing to believers, he says, "How great is the love the Father has lavished on us, that *we* should be called *children of God!* And that is what we are! The reason the *world* does not know *us* is that it did not know him."

There is, therefore, an abundant relationship between God the heavenly Father, and those who have become his children by faith in and obedience toward his Son. There is life, forgiveness, acceptance, inheritance, family, and discipline in this relationship. Yes, discipline; but our perfect and loving Father bestows even that discipline in order "that we may share in his holiness" (Heb. 12:10; cf. 12:4-11).

We must, moreover, observe that God is our Father "in heaven." That is the third observation about this designation. The Jews of Jesus' day were inclined, on the whole, to conceive of God as so exalted that personal relationships with him could scarcely be imagined. He was so transcendent that the richness of personality was frequently lost to view. By contrast, much modern evangelicalism tends to portray him as exclusively personal and warm. Somehow his sovereignty and exalted transcendence disappear. If you enter certain American churches you will hear the enthusiastic singing of some such ditty (I can scarcely grace it with "chorus") as "He's a great big wonderful God." Regrettably, I never fail to think of a great big wonderful teddy bear. Such "choruses" are not quite heretical, not quite blasphemous. I sometimes wish they were, for then they could be readily condemned for specific evil. They are something much worse than isolated blasphemy and heresy. They constitute part of a pattern of irreverence, shallow theology and experience-dominated religious criteria, which has eviscerated a terribly high proportion of evangelical strength in the Western world.

This does not contradict my earlier comments concerning the personal nature of God as portrayed by the designation "our Father." When Jesus taught his disciples to pray in this fashion, he was addressing men who were already convinced of the awesomeness of God's transcedence, the grandeur of God's ineffable exaltation. When they first timidly prayed, "Our Father in heaven," no doubt they deeply felt the tremendous privilege of approaching this marvelous God in so personal and intimate a fashion. But today, those who have lost sight of God's transcendence can no longer cherish the sheer privilege of addressing him as Father.

Fortunately, there are still believers who, with solemnity, meaning, and dignity, join together to sing some such praise as this:

> Immortal, invisible, God only wise,
> In light inaccessible hid from our eyes,
> Most blessed, most glorious, the Ancient of Days,
> Almighty, victorious, thy great name we praise.
>
> Great Father of glory, pure Father of light,
> Thine angels adore Thee, all veiling their sight;
> All laud we would render: O help us to see
> 'Tis only the splendour of light hideth Thee.
> *Walter Chalmers Smith (1824–1908)*

When such believers then pray, "Our Father in heaven," they cannot but be hushed and humbled.

With such a balanced opening, it is significant that the first petition concerns this exalted Father: "Hallowed be your name." In the semitic perspective, a person's name is closely related to what he is. Therefore, when God in the Old Testament reveals that he has this name or that, he is using his name to reveal himself as he is. The names are explanatory, they are revelatory. God's names include *God the Most High, Almighty, I am;* and compounds of the last one, which might be translated *I Am Who Is Our Help, I Am Who Is Our Righteousness.* And as we think of the character of God hidden behind these names, we are to pray, "Hallowed be your name."

"To hallow" means "to sanctify," to make holy, or to consider holy. The same verb is used in I Peter 3:15, where it would not be incorrect to translate, "But in your hearts hallow (or sanctify) Christ as the holy Lord." We are to reverence, honor, consider holy, and acknowledge

Christ as the holy Lord. Similarly we are to reverence, honor, consider holy, and acknowledge the name of God, and therefore God himself.

One intriguing aspect of this petition, I think, is that although it is a prayer that God's name be hallowed, and therefore presumably a request that God will hallow his own name, it is nevertheless a prayer which, when answered, means that *we* will hallow God's name. In other words, Christ's followers are asking their heavenly Father to act in such a way that they and an increasing number of others will reverence God, glorify him, consider him holy, and acknowledge him. Many men use "God" and "Jesus" as oaths, or as expressions of disgust or of anger, or in connection with jokes. But to the degree that this prayer is answered, not only will they put aside such habits, but they will regard God's name as so holy that the thought of it will be sufficient to incite a spirit of reverence and holy fear.

In a way, to pray, "Hallowed be your name" is to pray, "Make me holy. Grant that I may reverence you. Work in me and in other men so that we will acknowledge your unsurpassed and glorious holiness always." But the petition as Jesus teaches it is framed not so much in terms of what must happen to us for the prayer to be fulfilled, as in terms of the goal itself. The highest goal is not that we be made holy; the highest goal is rather that God's name be hallowed. This removes man from the center of the picture, and gives that place to God alone. Man—even transformed man—is not the chief goal of this universe. Man's chief *raison-d'être* is indeed, as the theologians have told us, to glorify God and to enjoy him forever. This one brief petition has so much meat in it for profitable meditation, so many implications about how we are to think about God, that it is sufficient in itself to drive us to our knees.

The second petition is no less brief: "Your kingdom come" (6:10). This cannot be a request that God's universal sovereignty will be exercised, for that is always in force. The reference is to God's saving reign, which, as we have seen, is in one sense already present, but which awaits the future for its consummation. To pray, "Your kingdom come," is to pray that God's saving reign will be expanded even now, and, much more, that God will usher in the consummated kingdom. When God's kingdom fully comes, it will do so because it is inaugurated by Jesus' return. If early Christians were eager for Jesus' power and authority to be manifested through them in their ongoing witness (see Acts 4:28f.), they were even more eager for Jesus' return, and prayed *"Marana tha!"*—"Come, O Lord!" (I Cor. 16:22). They were "looking forward to a new heaven and a new earth, the home of righteousness" (II Peter 3:13). The last book of the Bible concludes with the prayer, "Come, Lord Jesus" (Rev. 22:20).

"Your kingdom come." Christians ought not utter this petition lightly or thoughtlessly. Throughout the centuries, followers of Jesus suffering savage persecution have prayed this prayer with meaning and fervor. But I suspect that our comfortable pews often mock our sincerity when we repeat the phrase today. We would have no objection to the Lord's return, we think, provided he holds off a bit and lets us finish a degree first, or lets us taste marriage, or gives us time to succeed in a business or profession, or grants us the joy of seeing grandchildren. Do we really hunger for the kingdom to come in all its surpassing righteousness? Or would we rather waddle through a swamp of insincerity and unrighteousness?

The third petition broadens and somewhat specifies the boundaries of the second. "Your kingdom come" is followed by "Your will be done on earth as it is in heaven." This may well be a prayer that the kingdom of God might come in its fullness; for the most wonderful feature of that arrival will be the perfect accomplishment of the Father's will, without rebellion, prevarication, delay, evil agencies, and those mysterious twists by which God now works even through men's evil (see Gen. 50:20; Isa. 10:5-19).

The ambiguity of the language permits a broader application of this petition. God's ethical will (if I may use such an expression to speak of His desire to see righteousness practiced) will be completely fulfilled only in the consummated kingdom. But those who now belong to that kingdom, as that kingdom is at present manifest among us, are already under special obligation to fulfill that will. Much of Matthew 5 is saying just this: Surpassing righteousness is required to enter the kingdom (5:20). In the consummated kingdom, it will of course not be necessary to lay down guidelines about divorce, face-slapping, hate, lust, hypocrisy, and other foul things; but at present, an essential part of the pursuit of kingdom ethics is that such ethics must be worked out in a context in which evil still abounds. In the consummation, I shall not be tempted to retaliate against someone who slaps my face, because there will be no face-slapping; I shall not be tempted to hate my enemies, because I will have no enemies. Thus, although the absolute demands for righteousness are not diminished or diluted by appeal to the pressure of the present evil age, nevertheless they are framed in terms of opposition to the evil of the age. It is in this way that they point forward to the perfection of the consummated kingdom, when God's will shall be done openly, plainly, freely, without exceptions or caveats, *and without the painful necessity of framing it in terms of opposition to evil.*

Perhaps I can sum this up another way. When Jesus uses the phrase, "Your will be done *on earth* as it is *in heaven*," I think he chooses language which allows for several contrasts. He may be teaching us to pray

(1) that God's desires for righteousness will be as fully accomplished *now* on the earth as they are *now* accomplished in heaven; (2) that God's desires for righteousness may *ultimately* be as fully accomplished on the earth as they are *now* accomplished in heaven—i.e., this phrase is analogous to "Your kingdom come"; (3) that God's desires for righteousness may ultimately be accomplished on the earth *in the same way* that they are accomplished in heaven—that is, without reference to contrasting evil, but purely.

We need to realize that if we are praying that God's will be done on earth, we are committing ourselves to two important responsibilities. First of all, we are committing ourselves to learning all we can about his will. That means sustained and humble study of the Scriptures. It pains me to hear Christians insist on the authority and infallibility of the Scriptures, if those same Christians do not diligently work at learning the Scriptures. What are the themes of Zechariah and Galatians? What do we learn of God's will from Exodus and Ephesians? How do the portraits of Jesus painted by Matthew and John differ from and complement each other? In studying God's will, what have we learned this week that has prompted improvements in our lives?

That brings us to the second responsibility. If my heart hunger is that God's will be done, then praying this prayer is also my pledge that, so help me God, by his grace *I will do his will,* as much as I know it!

These are the three first petitions of the Lord's model prayer. The primary concerns and delights of Jesus' follower will be God's glory, God's reign, and God's will. After that, the Christian will take thought for the needs of himself and others.

The first petition in this connection is, "Give us today our daily bread" (6:11). The word translated "daily" occurs very rarely in Greek. In fact, it is found with one hundred percent certainty only in this prayer; but most likely it appears also in one of the papyri, which breaks off halfway through the word. It seems to be an adjective meaning "of the day that is coming." If in the morning we ask for our food for the day that is coming, we mean today's food; if we ask at night, we mean tomorrow's.

The point is the same in any case; and unfortunately, that point is lost in the complicated structures of contemporary Western society. In Jesus' day, laborers were commonly paid each day for the work they had achieved that day; and the pay was frequently so abysmally low that it was almost impossible to save any of it. Therefore the day's pay purchased the day's food. Moreover, the society was largely agrarian: one crop failure could spell a major disaster. In such a society, to pray "Give us today our daily bread" was no empty rhetoric. Living a relatively precarious existence, Jesus' followers were to learn to trust their heavenly Father to meet their physical needs.

But an even larger principle is at stake here. James, the half-brother of Jesus, reminds us, "Every good and perfect gift is from above, coming down from the Father of the heavenly lights, who does not change like shifting shadows" (James 1:17). Paul is more pungent: "For who makes you different from anyone else? What do you have that you did not receive? And if you did receive it, why do you boast as though you did not?" (I Cor. 4:7)—that is, as if you earned it, or grew it yourself. In other words, the Scriptures teach that God himself is the ultimate source of every good, whether food, clothing, work, leisure, strength, intelligence, friendship, or whatever. Moreover, he does not owe us these things. Since all of us have at some time or other gone our own tawdry way, effectively shaking our puny fists in his face and affirming our own independence, he would not be at all unjust were he to withhold his blessings. Our very ingratitude is an insult to Deity; the present thankless generation is an affront to him. We have taken his gifts for granted; and then when they begin to dry up we complain and call in question the very existence of this beneficent God.

Life in Western society is not quite as precarious as it was in the first century. We have received so much more. But sadly, our very wealth has contributed to our thanklessness, to our spiritual bankruptcy. As I pen these lines, news is pouring in of drought in Europe, Australia, and elsewhere. I would not want to argue that Europe is more evil than the rest of the world; rather, I wonder if God is beginning to call to the Western world in the terrible language of judgment, until we learn some lessons of repentance, gratitude, poverty of spirit, and perhaps more than anything else, conscious dependence on him.

If difficult times do descend on us, it is the follower of Jesus who will find refuge in this petition, "Give us today our daily bread" (Matt. 6:11). Nor is it simply a question of praying such a prayer in order to teach us dependence on God, although it is partly that. Rather, the annals of Christian experience overflow with the witness that God is able to answer such a petition in the most faithful way.*

The second petition is found in verse 12: "Forgive us our debts, as we also have forgiven our debtors." Jesus goes on to enlarge the point after he has finished his model prayer, for in verses 14f. he adds, "For if you forgive men when they sin against you, your heavenly Father will also forgive you. But if you do not forgive men their sins, your Father will not forgive your sins." Sin is pictured in the prayer as a debt. Sin incurs a debt which must be discharged. If then someone owes us such a debt, and we fail to release him by forgiving him, our own debts before the

---

*Perhaps the most remarkable narrative in this connection is the biography *George Müller of Bristol*, by A. T. Pierson.

Father will not be forgiven by him, and we will not be released. Actually, in Aramaic, which is the language Jesus probably used in preaching this sermon, it is not uncommon to refer to sin as a debt.

Is Jesus giving us some tit-for-tat arrangement here? Do I forgive Johnny and then the Lord forgives me—indeed, *so that* the Lord will forgive me? The New International Version (hereafter called NIV) of verse 12 strengthens such an interpretation, although the Greek behind it may simply mean "as we herewith forgive our debtors," and not necessarily "as we also have forgiven our debtors." But what then do the very explicit conditions of verses 14 and 15 mean?

Some light is shed on the passage by a parable Jesus tells in Matthew 18:23-35:

> 23"Therefore, the kingdom of heaven is like a king who wanted to settle accounts with his servants. 24As he began the settlement, a man who owed him ten thousand talents was brought to him. 25Since he was not able to pay, the master ordered that he and his wife and children and all that he had be sold to repay the debt.
>
> 26"The servant fell on his knees before him. 'Be patient with me,' he begged, 'and I will pay back everything.' 27The servant's master took pity on him, cancelled the debt and let him go.
>
> 28"But when that servant went out, he found one of his fellow servants who owed him a hundred denarii. He grabbed him and began to choke him. 'Pay back what you owe me!' he demanded.
>
> 29"His fellow servant fell to his knees and begged him, 'Be patient with me, and I will pay you back.'
>
> 30"But he refused. Instead, he went off and had the man thrown in prison until he could pay the debt. 31When the other servants saw what had happened, they were greatly distressed and went and told their master everything that had happened.
>
> 32"Then the master called the servant in. 'You wicked servant,' he said, 'I cancelled all that debt of yours because you begged me to. 33Shouldn't you have had mercy on your fellow servant just as I had on you?' 34In anger his master turned him over to the jailers until he paid back all he owed.
>
> 35"This is how my heavenly Father will treat each of you unless you forgive your brother from your heart."

The point of the parable it seems does not so much turn on temporal sequence (X must forgive Y before Z can forgive X) as on attitude. There is no forgiveness for the one who does not forgive. How could it be otherwise? His unforgiving spirit bears strong witness to the fact that he has never repented.

It is of the essence of the Christian way to walk in self-denial. Whoever sees himself and his own life as central to meaningful existence loses everything; whoever takes up his cross, follows Christ, and loses his life, actually finds it. In this sense, the famous prayer attributed to St.

Francis of Assisi explores the categories by which this petition in the Lord's model prayer is to be understood:

> Lord, make me an instrument of your peace.
>   Where there is hatred, let me sow love;
>   where there is injury, pardon;
>   where there is doubt, faith;
>   where there is despair, hope;
>   where there is darkness, light;
>   and where there is sadness, joy.
>
> O Divine Master, grant that I may not so much seek
>   to be consoled as to console,
>   to be understood as to understand,
>   to be loved as to love.
>
> For it is in giving that we receive,
>   it is in pardoning that we are pardoned,
>   and it is in dying that we are born to eternal life.

The final petition of the prayer is this: "And lead us not into temptation, but deliver us from the evil one" (6:13). At first sight this is a very strange request. Why should we have to ask God *not* to lead us into temptation? Couldn't we take that for granted? To ask God to keep us out of temptation would be more understandable; but to ask that he not lead us into it is difficult.

Many pages have been written on this petition, but I suspect the real explanation of this puzzling phrase is simpler than most of the proposed solutions. I think this is a *litotes*, a figure of speech which expresses something by negating the contrary. For example, "not a few" means "many"; by negating "a few" we have produced this litotes. In John 6:37, Jesus says, "All that the Father gives me will come to me, *and whoever comes to me I will never drive away.*" Many people think the latter clause is a litotes meaning, "I will certainly receive all who come to me." In fact, it is an even stronger litotes than that. As the succeeding verses clearly show, it means "I will certainly keep in all who come to me." Thus, by negating "drive away," a forceful and somewhat ironic expression for "keep in" is generated.

It appears to me that "Lead us not into temptation" is a litotes akin to these examples. "Into temptation" is negated: Lead us, *not* into temptation, but away from it, into righteousness, into situations where, far from being tempted, we will be protected and therefore kept righteous. As the second clause of this petition expresses it, we will then be delivered from the evil one.

This petition is a hefty reminder that, just as we ought consciously to depend on God for physical sustenance, so also ought we to sense our dependence on him for moral triumph and spiritual victory. Indeed, to fail in this regard is already to have fallen, for it is part of that ugly effort at independence which refuses to recognize our position as creatures before God. As Christians grow in holy living, they sense their own inherent moral weakness and rejoice that whatever virtue they possess flourishes as the fruit of the Spirit. More and more they recognize the deceptive subtleties of their own hearts, and the malicious cunning of the evil one, and fervently request of their heavenly Father, "Lead us not into temptation, but deliver us from evil."

When did you last pray such a prayer? Is it not a mark of spiritual carelessness, and insensitivity to the spiritual dimensions of human existence, when such prayers are neglected?

The fact that the plea to avoid temptation is placed between the petition concerning forgiveness (6:12) and its further elucidation (6:14f.) may possibly suggest that the temptation primarily in view is the temptation to be bitter, the temptation to maintain a veneer of true religion even while one's secret attitudes are bursting with the corruption of grapes gone sour. This also suits the dominant theme of this passage (6:1-18), the description and overthrow of religious hypocrisy.

The doxology printed in some English versions ("for yours is the kingdom and the power and the glory forever. Amen.") appears not to have been added before the late second century, at the earliest. This observation does not call into question the fact that the kingdom and the power and the glory really do belong to God forever; many other passages say similar things. However, it remains doubtful that Jesus taught such a clause as part of his model prayer.

There is so much to be learned about praying; most of us are little more than novices. One of the most profitable studies of the Scripture is the examination of the prayers recorded in its pages. Then, of course, the student needs to practice what he has discovered. But, regardless how many riches he finds, he will not come across a prayer more all-encompassing, more pointed, more *exemplary*, than the Lord's model prayer.

Blessed is the follower of Jesus who can sing, without embarrassment, insincerity, or a trace of a blush (despite the quaintness of some of the wording):

> Sweet hour of prayer! Sweet hour of prayer!
> That calls me from a world of care,
> And bids me at my Father's throne
> Make all my wants and wishes known.
> In seasons of distress and grief

My soul has often found relief,
And oft escaped the tempter's snare
By thy return, sweet hour of prayer.

Sweet hour of prayer! Sweet hour of prayer!
Thy wings shall my petition bear
To him whose truth and faithfulness
Engage my waiting soul to bless.
And since he bids me seek his face,
Believe his word and trust his grace,
I'll cast on him my every care,
And wait for thee, sweet hour of prayer.
William W. Walford (1772–1850)

Fasting, 6:16-18

Jesus' third example of ostentatious piety is fasting. "When you fast,"
he says, "do not look sombre as the hypocrites do, for they disfigure
their faces to show men they are fasting. I tell you the truth, they have
received their reward in full" (6:16). Just as Jesus did not demean
almsgiving and prayer, so likewise does he refrain from speaking against
fasting *per se:* he assumes his disciples will fast. On the other hand, in
another context he is found defending his disciples for *not* fasting,
(Matthew 9:14-17.) In any case, here in the Sermon on the Mount Jesus
is interested in condemning the abuses of the practice, and in exposing
its dangers.

In the Jewish calendar there were certain special fasts in which every-
body participated. These took place in connection with the high feast
days, such as the Day of Atonement or the Jewish New Year. Fasts
might also be called when, for example, the autumn rains failed to appear; these fasts, too, would be national in scope. In addition, many individuals would fast at other times, allegedly for reasons of moral and
religious self-discipline, and especially as a sign of deep repentance and
brokenness before the Lord, and perhaps as part of some important request offered up to the Lord.

But what began as spiritual self-discipline was prostituted into an occasion for pompous self-righteousness. Some would wear glum and
pained expressions on their faces, go about their business unwashed and
unkempt, and sprinkle ashes on their head, all to inform peers that they
were fasting. What was once a sign of humiliation became a sign of self-
righteous self-display.

Tragically, we do similar things today. At one time people wore nice
clothes on Sunday as a sign of respect and reverence before the Lord. It

was not long before the quality of the clothes became more important than the reverence; and pretty soon people were competing to look better than their neighbors. Small wonder many youths finally rejected every trace of this clothes contest and started wearing blue jeans to church. Many of them may have done so for unworthy motives, but their parents' motives for dressing up were equally unworthy.

In one campus outreach group, Christian students were strongly urged to carry their Bibles to school and college as a sign of their faith and a witness to others. After all, if they were not embarrassed to carry Freud or a chemistry text or a novel, why should they balk at carrying their Bibles? But pretty soon I noticed some Christians were carrying exceptionally *big* Bibles. . . . Like hypocrites in Jesus' day, they were trying to establish a reputation for piety.

Almost anything that is supposed to serve as an outward sign of an inward attitude can be cheapened by this hypocritical piety. Jesus told those who wanted to fast, "But when you fast, put oil on your head and wash your face, so that it will not be obvious to men that you are fasting, but only to your Father, who is unseen; and your Father, who sees what is done in secret, will reward you" (6:17f.). Jesus is telling his followers that when they fast they are to act normally so that no one but God will know it. They are to take off the ashes, wash their faces, use their deodorant or talc or oil or whatever, and act normally. No voluntary act of spiritual discipline is ever to become an occasion for self-promotion. Otherwise, any value to the act is utterly vitiated.

The thrust of Matthew 6:1-18 is humbling. Matthew five's demand for righteousness is now complemented by the insistence that such righteousness must never become confused with pious ostentation, with play-acting piety. The question is raised in its most practical form: Whom am I trying to please by my religious practices? Honest reflection on that question can produce most disquieting results. If it does, then a large part of the solution is to start practicing piety in the secret intimacy of the Lord's presence. If our "acts of righteousness" are not primarily done secretly before him, then secretly they may be done to please men.

The negatives of these verses are actually an important way of getting to the supreme positive, namely, transparent righteousness. Genuine godliness, unaffected holiness, unfeigned piety—these are superlatively clean, superlatively attractive. The real beauty of righteousness must not be tarnished by sham.

God help us.

4 MATTHEW 6:19-34

KINGDOM PERSPECTIVES

The first part of Matthew 6, as we saw in the last chapter, confounds hypocrisy. As such, it is largely negative in tone; yet by that negative tone the positive lesson is driven home. In the pursuit of the righteousness of the kingdom, a man must make sure that his specifically religious "acts of righteousness" are preserved from hypocrisy. He can best avoid hypocrisy by guaranteeing that his ultimate objective is to please God and be rewarded by him. In practical terms, he must eschew all showiness in acts of piety.

At stake are the perspectives of the kingdom. Life in the kingdom is not simply a question of crossing one hurdle or passing one test, followed by relative indifference to kingdom norms. Involved, rather, is that deep repentance which willingly orients all of life around these norms. The second half of Matthew 6, therefore, builds on what has come before. Followers of Jesus not only shun hypocrisy in religious duty, but, more positively, they comprehend that all of life is to be lived and all its attitudes are to be formed according to the perspectives of the kingdom.

Jesus enunciates two general but all-embracing kingdom perspectives. The first is unswerving loyalty to kingdom values, and the second is uncompromised trust in God.

UNSWERVING LOYALTY TO KINGDOM VALUES
Three Metaphors
Matthew 6:19-24

Treasure, 6:19-21

"Do not store up for yourselves treasures on earth, where moth and rust destroy, and where thieves break in and steal. But store up for yourselves treasures in heaven, where moth and rust do not destroy, and where thieves do not break in and steal. For where your treasure is, there your heart will be also." The treasures on earth here envisaged clearly include rich oriental garments, the sort of clothing any self-respecting moth would dearly love to find. The word translated "rust" may mean just that, and therefore be connected with the corrosion of metals; but it can refer to other kinds of decay and destruction as well. For example, it can refer to something which eats away at a supply of grain. Older commentators, rightly I think, picture a farm along with its products and supplies being eroded, corroded, fouled, destroyed.

Even valuables which cannot be corroded or eaten can be stolen. Many "treasures of earth" are the delight of thieves, who break in and steal. Actually, they "dig through" and steal; for most homes in ancient Palestine were made of mud brick which easily succumbed to any thief with a sharp tool.

In principle, by "treasures of earth" Jesus refers to any valuable which is perishable or which can be lost in one way or another. The means by which the treasure is lost is unimportant (but in our day certainly includes galloping inflation).

By contrast, followers of Jesus must store up for themselves treasures in heaven, where moth and rust do not destroy, where thieves do not break in and steal—and where inflation cannot possibly operate. The treasures in question are things which are the result of the divine approval and which will be lavished upon the disciples in the consummated kingdom. The treasures of the new heaven and the new earth are wonderful beyond our wildest expectation. Sometimes the pages of Scripture give us glimpses couched in glittering metaphor as the resources of language are called up to tell us of things still barely conceivable. At other times Scripture extrapolates the advance tastes we enjoy here, and pictures love undiluted, a way of life utterly sinless, integrity untarnished, work and responsibility without fatigue, deep emotions without tears, worship without restraint or disharmony or sham, and best of all the presence of God in an unqualified and unrestricted and personal way. Such treasures cannot be assailed by corrosion or theft.

I do not think that Jesus is condemning all wealth, any more than he is condemning all clothes. He is not prohibiting things, but the love of things. Not money, but the love of money, is a root of all kinds of evil (I Tim. 6:10). Jesus forbids us from making mere things our treasure, storing things up as if they had ultimate importance.

The preacher, Ecclesiastes, can help us here. Ecclesiastes pictures the construction of buildings, the work ethic, sex, reputation, power, various philosophies, and then dismisses each of them as vanity and a striving after wind. My friend and colleague Dr. Harold Dressler has convinced me that the word translated "vanity" is not to be taken to mean that all these things are equally useless, stupid, "vain," but that all these things are transient. They are "vanity" in the sense that they are non-enduring. Such things, if you will, are cursed with temporality, with transience. When I die, I will take out with me exactly what I brought in—nothing. Therefore even if thieves and rust spare my goods for the span of my life, it is vain to store up treasures which have such time-limited value.

Of course, to argue as Jesus here argues presupposes belief in rewards and punishments from heaven. Therefore only the man of faith will acknowledge that the argument is valid; for as the writer of the Epistle to the Hebrews puts it, "Without faith it is impossible to please God, because anyone who comes to him must believe that he exists and that he rewards those who earnestly seek him" (Heb. 11:6). But if I am genuinely committed to the kingdom of God, my most cherished values will be established by God.

Just as the kingdom is already present, at least incipiently, so even now the disciple of Jesus is accumulating, and enjoying, treasure in heaven. And just as the kingdom is still to come in the fullness of its splendor, so also the disciple of Jesus awaits that consummation in order to enter the fullness of the blessings the Father has prepared for him. He lives by faith; but granted the reality of the objects of that faith, the restraints here expounded are reasonable. We must ask ourselves (if once again I may refer to eternity in the categories of time) how important contemporary transient values will appear to us in fifty billion trillion millennia. It is a poor bargain which exchanges the eternal for the temporal, regardless of how much tinsel is used to make the temporal more attractive. And it is tragic if we have to follow the examples of Achan, Solomon, the rich young ruler, and Demas, in order to discover this basic truth for ourselves.

It is not merely a question of ultimate rewards. It is much more than that, for the things we treasure actually govern our lives. What we value tugs at our minds and emotions; it consumes our time with planning, day-dreaming, and effort to achieve. As Jesus puts it, "For where your treasure is, there your heart will be also." If a man wants *above all else* to make a lot of money, buy an extravagant house, ski in the Alps or sail in the Mediterranean, head up his company or buy out his competitor, build his reputation or achieve that next promotion, advance a political opinion or seek public office, he will be devoured by these goals, and the values of the kingdom will get squeezed out. Notice that none of the goals I mentioned is intrinsically bad; but none is of ultimate value, either. Therefore any of them can *become* evil if it is valued as ultimate treasure and thereby usurps the place of the kingdom. And how much uglier is the situation when the goals *are* positively evil! But the principle remains the same: We think about our treasures, we are drawn toward our treasures, we fret about our treasures, we measure other things (and other people) by our treasures. This is so painfully true that a person who honestly examines himself can pretty well discover what his real treasures are, simply by studying his deepest desires.

In Canada, freshly fallen snow is usually dry and powdery, not wet and sticky. A large field of new snow is so inviting as it glistens in the winter sun. No mark is on it, no footprint; yours is the privilege of tramping across it and establishing any pattern you like. If you look fixedly at your feet and try to cross the field in a straight line, you will make a most erratic pattern. If instead, you fix your eye on a tree or boulder on the other side and walk straight toward it, the path you leave will be quite remarkably straight.

While we were engaged to be married, Joy and I lived in Cambridge, England. Sometimes we enjoyed long bicycle rides together along the tow path beside the river Cam. Pedaling along, I was never more than two or three feet from the sharp bank: an accidental swerve would mean a tumble into the river. Where the path is wide enough to ride two abreast, Joy would be on the inside. If in conversing back and forth she then started to look at me, I would have to slam on my brakes to avoid either tangling with her bicycle or being forced into the river.

Such illustrations teach us that we tend to move toward the object on which we fix our gaze. In the same way, our whole lives drift relentlessly toward the spot where our treasures are stored, because our hearts will take us there. To follow Jesus faithfully entails therefore a consistent development of our deepest loves, to train ourselves to adopt an unswerving loyalty to kingdom values and to delight in all that God approves. Small wonder that Paul writes in these terms: "Since, then, you have been raised with Christ, set your hearts on things above, where Christ is seated at the right hand of God. Set your minds on things above, not on earthly things" (Col. 3:1f.). Or again: "Command those who are rich in this present world not to be arrogant nor to put their hope in wealth, which is so uncertain, but to put their hope in God, who richly provides us with everything for our enjoyment. Command them to do good, to be rich in good deeds, and to be generous and willing to share. *In this way they will lay up treasure for themselves as a firm foundation for the coming age,* so that they may take hold of the life that is truly life" (I Tim. 6:17-19).

Light, 6:22f.

The next metaphor is a little more difficult to understand. Jesus says, "The eye is the lamp of the body. If your eyes are good, your whole body will be full of light. But if your eyes are bad, your whole body will be full of darkness. If then the light within you is darkness, how great is that darkness!"

It is possible that this thought has its roots in the preceding paragraph. If so, the eye is the lamp of the body in the sense that it enables the body to find its way. Your eye must be "good," in order for it to direct "your whole body" (a semitic expression meaning "you yourself") toward what is good.

Alternatively, it is possible (and in my judgment, preferable) to interpret verses 22f. in a somewhat simpler fashion. The whole body—that is, the whole person—is pictured as a room or a house. The purpose of the eye is to illuminate this room, to ensure that it is "full of light." The eye thus serves as the source of light; we might think of a window in an otherwise windowless room, although in fact Jesus uses the figure of a lamp, not a window.

For the individual to be full of light, then, the eyes must be "good." If they are bad, if their flame is smoky or their glass caked with soot, if their wick is untrimmed or their fuel depleted, the person remains in utter darkness. Clearly, it is important to discover just what Jesus means, in non-metaphorical terms, by demanding that the eye be "good."

But this adjective "good" is a little perplexing. The word in the original was used in the Septuagint to mean "singleness of purpose, undivided loyalty": hence "single" in the King James Version. However, among the rabbis, the "evil eye" indicated selfishness; and in that case the good eye might well indicate committed generosity. Being full of light is equivalent to being generous; and that seems to fit in well enough as an elaboration of the preceding paragraph's warnings about foolishly selected treasure.

I suggest that the Septuagint meaning of the word is best, if we may judge by the context. Although at first glance the alternative idea concerning generosity seems to mesh well with the preceding paragraph's interest in treasure and the next paragraph's warning against money, closer inspection reveals that the fit is not so good. Verses 19-20 are less concerned with financial wealth and giving it away than with a man's scale of values whereby he establishes what is his ultimate treasure. Similarly, verse 24 is not so much focused on money as it is on servitude and commitment.

In other words, verses 19-21 and verse 24 all demand unswerving loyalty to kingdom values; the particulars used are treasure and money. The accent remains on singleness of purpose—heart fidelity—toward God. Therefore the word translated "good" by the NIV most probably means "singleness of purpose, undivided loyalty"—which, context apart, is the most natural interpretation. The good eye is the one fixed on God, unwavering in its gaze, constant in its fixation.

The result is that the entire person is "full of light." I think this expression is lovely. If light is taken in its usual connotations of revelation and purity, then the individual with a single eye toward kingdom values is the person characterized by maximum understanding of divinely revealed truth and by unabashedly pure behavior. Moreover, the expression "full of light" is probably not limited to what the person is in himself, isolated; but that person will also be so full of light that he will *give off* light. It is by this unreserved commitment to kingdom values that Christians become "the light of the world" (Matt. 5:14).

The alternative is to be "full of darkness," devoid of revelation and purity. That darkness is especially appalling if the person deceives himself. If he thinks his eye is good when it is bad, he talks himself into believing that his nominal loyalty to kingdom values is deep and genuine, when in fact it is shallow and contrived. That person's darkness is greatest who thinks his darkness is light: "If then the light within you is darkness, how great is that darkness!"

Slavery, 6:24

"No one can serve two masters. Either he will hate the one and love the other, or he will be devoted to the one and despise the other. You cannot serve both God and Money" (6:24).

Superficially, the text appears somewhat extreme in its polarization. But two things must be kept in mind if we are to understand it correctly. First, by "masters" Jesus does not have twentieth-century employers in mind (most of whom are limited in authority by trade unions), but something closer to slave owners (although perhaps not quite that stereotyped). It is possible to work for two employers; it is not so easy to serve two masters.

Second, the contrast between love and hate is a common semitic idiom, neither part of which may legitimately be taken absolutely. To hate one of two alternatives and to love the other simply means the latter is strongly preferred, especially if there is any contest between the two. This idiom sheds light on other words of Jesus: "If anyone comes to me and does not hate his father and mother, his wife and children, his brothers and sisters—yes, even his own life—he cannot be my disciple" (Luke 14:26). This same Jesus elsewhere insists that people should honor their parents with integrity (Mark 7:9-13); so clearly, he is not advocating hatred. He means that any man's best love and first allegiance must be directed toward the Father and toward the Son whom he sent, and that even family ties must be considered secondary.

In the same way, Matthew 6:24 warns us that during crises our allegiances get sorted out, and only one can come out on top. One "master" will be preferred: what or whom we want to serve most will be revealed. And then Jesus gives us one pithy example: "You cannot serve both God and Money."

The word translated "Money" in the NIV is transliterated in most other versions as "Mammon." Orginally the word meant "something in ✓ which one puts confidence," or the like. Eventually, no doubt because man's confidence is so often deposited in riches, the word came to refer to all material possessions: profit, wealth, money. No one can be simultaneously devoted to both God and money.

Let us admit it. Many, many of us try very hard to compromise in this area. Two jobs become available, and for most of us the weightiest factor prompting us to select the one or the other will be the salary, not the opportunity presented by each option to serve the Lord. Or we make a needless move to a bigger and better car or a bigger and better home, for no other reason than to keep up with (or surpass) peers.

Contrast the attitude of the commentator Matthew Henry (1662-1714) who, when he was robbed, returned home and wrote in his diary words to this effect:

> Lord, I thank you
> that I have never been robbed before;
> that although they took my money, they spared my life;
> that although they took everything, it wasn't very much;
> that it was I who was robbed, not I who robbed.

Matthew Henry was a man who served God.

These three metaphors—treasure, light, and slavery—join forces to demand unswerving loyalty to kingdom values.

UNCOMPROMISED TRUST
Matthew 6:25-34

"Therefore I tell you, do not worry about your life, what you will eat or drink; or about your body, what you will wear. Is not life more important than food, and the body more important than clothes?" What is the "Therefore" there for? It is a logical connective directing attention to what has preceded: *Because* transient earthly treasures do not satisfy and do not last (6:19-21), *because* moral and spiritual vision is easily distorted and darkened (6:22f.), *because* a choice must be made between God and Money (6:24), *because* the kingdom of God demands unswerving allegiance to its values (6:19-24), *therefore* do not worry, and in particular do not worry about mere things.

But let us consider a more subtle connection. Jesus has been minimizing the ultimate significance of material possessions; and no doubt not a few among his hearers find themselves wondering, "But what about necessities? It's all very well to turn your back on wealth when you're rich; but I've got a wife and children, and I can barely provide them with food, clothing, and shelter. What are you saying to me?" In effect, Jesus answers that just as earthly possessions can become an idol which deposes God by becoming disproportionately important, so also can earthly needs become a source of worry which deposes God by fostering distrust. Loyalty to kingdom values rejects all subservience to temporal things, whether that subservience be the type which accumulates endlessly, or the type stamped by a frenetic, faithless, and worried scurry for essentials.

*   *   *

Before examining what Matthew 6:25-34 says about worry, I think it wise to make some general observations about worry and the response of the New Testament to it. This is because anxiety and tension have become a major point of discussion in our society, and attitudes toward it have degenerated into several polarized positions. It is necessary to make an appeal for balance and caution.

Picture three people. The first is a happy-go-lucky, cheerful, almost irresponsible person. He rarely gets anything done, and never gets anything done on time. He doesn't worry about the next five minutes, let alone tomorrow. Responsibility he wears too lightly; life is a lark. If he is a Christian, it is very difficult to get him to work faithfully at any task. He probably won't cause any tension by stooping to bitterness or vindictiveness: everyone knows him as a "nice guy." On the other hand, he remains insensitive to the needs and feelings of others, and is consistently carefree about the spiritual lostness of millions of men.

The second person is almost hyper-responsible. He takes every grief and burden seriously. If there is any trouble, he frets so much over it that he produces outsize ulcers. The state of the economy is a constant weight on his mind: not only does he worry about tomorrow, he wonders how he'll make out when he retires in forty-two years. He may spread the objects of his worry around, so that every bit of bad news, or even a whiff of potentially bad news, prompts a new outbreak of anxiety; or he may focus his worry and inflated sense of responsibility on a few restricted areas, with the result that he utterly excludes other people and topics.

The third person is a balanced and sane young Christian, noteworthy for his integrity and disciplined hard work. Married with two children, he is supporting them faithfully while he tries to finish his doctorate. With about one year to go, he wakes one night to discover that his wife can't speak and can't move her right side. A brain tumor is discovered; but major surgery proves useless. The doctor tells the young man that the recovery period will be lengthy, and will not return his wife to normal strength and mental clarity in any case. In fact, the prognosis is three years, during which time she will become more and more like a vegetable; and then she will die.

These three people hear some preacher use Matthew 6:25-34 as the basis for a long sermon on the wickedness of worry. The preacher says that worry involves distrust in God, and this is shameful.

How will each react?

The first will be quite happy. He always knew that other people were too uptight all the time. Why bother studying so hard for an "A"? Just passing the course is good enough. Why get so hung up with binding commitments? He's happy and free, and cheerfully obeying the Lord's injunction not to worry.

The second may feel quite rebuked by the sermon. He knows it is for him. He worries that he has been denying the Lord, and despairs of himself and his sins. Quite without any sense of irony, he begins to worry about worry.

The third person listens to the sermon, and, unless he is remarkably mature and full of grace, bitterly sneers under his breath something to the effect that the preacher should watch his own wife die before venturing on so difficult a subject. And if this third man is tired and feeling a trifle vindictive, he may start to tick off on his mental fingers a few of the things that somebody jolly well *ought* to start worrying about: ecological problems, threat of nuclear holocaust, runaway inflation, widely scattered wars, racial prejudice, totalitarian cruelty, economic oppression, rampaging alcoholism in France and rampaging venereal disease in America. He may also list other more personal problems: divorce, competition for promotion at work, deadlines, family feuding, rebellious teenagers, and so on. These personal frustrations and enmities somehow coalesce with national and international concerns because they are all deposited in our minds by newspapers, radio, and television. Not worry? Man number three hears such an injunction and weighs it against the gnawing anxieties which plague the spirit and endanger health, and he mutters, "You don't understand. It can't be done."

These three represent only a small number of possible reactions, but they illustrate the kind of problem this exposition of the text has confronted again and again. Interpreting the Scriptures demands both balance and precision: balance to weld together diverse teachings, and precision so that no one teaching is thoughtlessly extrapolated out of proportion.

Moreover, the application of these diverse emphases requires a certain pastoral awareness of the needs of each individual. The first man needs to hear something about discipline, self-sacrifice, and hard work, and he needs to have illegitimate worry differentiated from these. The second man ought to hear of God's providence, of the means and results of prayer, and of the self-centeredness which is frequently a large constituent of nagging worry. The third man needs to have a close and loving brother weep with him, pledge support, and perhaps point afresh to the final proof of divine benevolence, the cross of Christ.

I shall offer two propositions:

(1) There is a sense in which worry is not only good, but its absence is, biblically speaking, irresponsible.

(2) There is a sense in which worry is not only evil, but its presence signifies unbelief and disobedience.

The first sort of "worry" is simply the concern of the follower of Jesus to be faithful and useful in his master's service. Even a casual reading of the Pauline corpus makes it clear that Paul lived and ministered with a certain intensity, a throbbing commitment not only to become more Christ-like himself, but also to fight spiritual battles on behalf of an exponentially-increasing number of other believers. His commitment cost him the hardship and sufferings detailed in II Corinthians 11:23ff. "Besides everything else," Paul adds, "I face the daily pressure of my concern for all the churches. Who is weak, and I do not feel weak? Who is led into sin, and I do not inwardly burn?" (II Cor. 11:28f.).

In addition to these concerns the Christian can be greatly exercised concerning sin, as the beatitudes themselves testify (cf. also Ps. 38 and 51). Small wonder the Christian way can be described in terms of wrestling, boxing; or as a fight, a struggle, a race that demands every effort if the goal is to be reached and the prize won. There is little justification in Scripture for picturing the Christian life in terms of constantly effervescent joy, unbounded peace, unbroken serenity; and still less is there warrant for irresponsibility toward the Lord in the use of his gifts. Joy and peace and freedom there are, but only within the matrix of unadulterated commitment to Jesus, along with all the pressures such commitment must inevitably bring.

None of these "worries" is purely selfish. Moreover, such concerns (a less emotive term than "worries") are essentially God-directed. That is, they are a result of looking at things from God's perspective, and seeking to ensure that his will be done on earth as it is in heaven. The absence of such "worries" is irresponsible.

On the other hand, many worries are both illicit and harmful. There is nothing wrong with puttering about the kitchen; but if commitment to the kitchen prompts impatience and distorted values, it deserves rebuke (Luke 10:38-42). Some seed gets planted and grows in a most promising way at first, before thorn bushes choke the life out of it; and those thorn bushes are "the worries of this life and the deceitfulness of wealth" (Matt. 13:22). We sense Paul's desire to eliminate corrupting worry in Philippians 4:6f.: "Do not be anxious about anything, but in everything, by prayer and petition, with thanksgiving, present your requests to God. And the peace of God, which transcends all understanding, will guard your hearts and your minds in Christ Jesus." Too many Christians overlook the fact that the apostle here gives us the *means* of overcoming worry, as well as his prohibition.

I dare not neglect prayer and thanksgiving if I am to enjoy God's transcendent peace and overcome my worries. I must abhor thankless bitterness and eschew sulkiness. My worries must be enumerated before the Father, along with thoughtful requests framed in accordance with his will. These requests must be offered to the accompaniment of sincere gratitude for the many undeserved blessings already received, and for the privilege of stretching my faith by exposure to this new and improved hardship. Thus the follower of Jesus learns really to trust the all-wise and all-gracious sovereignty of God (Rom. 8:28), as he begins to experience the profundity of Peter's injunction: "Humble yourselves, therefore, under God's mighty hand, that he may lift you up in due time. Cast all your anxiety on him because he cares for you" (I Peter 5:6f.).

Most—if not all—illicit worries indicate an acute shortage of confidence in God; and therefore to some extent they are self-centered. Most are bound to temporal categories; and where they are not, as in the fearful brother who fears God's grace is insufficient to pardon him, all the rich promises of the gospel are available to quell them.

Perhaps the trickiest forms of worry are those which marry legitimate concern with self-centered worry. For example, the preacher may be honestly exercised about an impending address he is to give, that it be true, helpful, anointed by the Spirit of God, and spoken in love. But he may also be worried about his reputation. We humans are very skilled at developing mixed motives and mixed worries. God help us to reinforce the good and hold the evil in abomination.

❋   ❋   ❋

With what sort of worry is our Lord concerned in Matthew 6:25-34? Quite clearly, he is not advocating carefree irresponsibility. What he teaches is that even material necessities are not valid causes of worry among the heirs of the kingdom. Therefore our physical needs, however legitimate they may be, must never supplant our prior commitment to the kingdom of God and his righteousness. Furthermore, he teaches that these same needs become opportunities for living a life distinctive from the surrounding pagans who never learn to trust God for even the basic necessities.

The general principle, 6:25

"Therefore I tell you, do not worry about your life, what you will eat or drink; or about your body, what you will wear. Is not life more important than food, and the body more important than clothes?" The New International Version's "Do not worry" is superior to the King James Version's "Take no thought," since the injunction is not designed to promote thoughtlessness, but freedom from care.

There is an implicit *a fortiori* argument here. An *a fortiori* argument is one with the form, "If this, then how much more that?" There are some famous examples of such reasoning in the New Testament. Perhaps the best known is Romans 8:32: "He who did not spare his own Son, but gave him up for us all—how will he not also, along with him, graciously give us all things?" God has already given us his best gift; how much more will he give us lesser gifts! Another excellent example of an *a fortiori* argument lies in the chapter under study: "If that is how God clothes the grass of the field, which is here today and tomorrow is thrown into the fire, will he not much more clothe you, O you of little faith?" (Matt. 6:30). Again, in Matthew 7:11 we find: "If you, then, though you are evil, know how to give good gifts to your children, how much more will your Father in heaven give good gifts to those who ask him!"

In Matthew 6:25, the *a fortiori* argument is only implicit, because the form isn't present; but the thought seems to be something like this: he who provides us with life, with bodies (which from our perspective are most important), how much more will he also provide things of lesser importance like food and clothes! Therefore, the follower of Jesus is not to worry about such needs, as basic as they are.

This point is driven home by two examples.

Two examples, 6:26-30

Life and food, 6:26f.

"Look at the birds of the air; they do not sow or reap or store away in barns, and yet your heavenly Father feeds them. Are you not much more valuable than they? Who of you by worrying can add a single hour to his life?"

During three enjoyable years in Cambridge, England, I spent most of my time working in the excellent facilities of the Tyndale Library. Outside the window by my desk stretched a pleasant, well-kept garden. Every morning, and often throughout the day, scores of birds would come to scratch and peck and pull up worms. But for all their constant activity, they seemed carefree and alert; they chirped and sang, the high note of the robin mingling with the more mellow warble of the thrush and the common note of the sparrow.

These creatures live from day to day, "they do not sow or reap or store away in barns." Jesus, however, is not arguing that they should be our paradigm, and that we should therefore abolish farming. Rather, he goes on to tell us that despite the day-to-day kind of existence among birds, "yet your heavenly Father feeds them." The conclusion is inevitable: "Are you not much more valuable than they?" If your heavenly Father feeds them, will he not undertake to feed you, especially in the light of the fact that he considers you more valuable than they? And therefore is not constant worry about how future meals will be provided an affront to God, a charge that we cannot trust his providence? Has not Jesus already taught the heirs of the kingdom to pray, "Give us today our daily bread"? And will this prayer, taught by Jesus himself, be mocked by the Almighty?

Jesus' argument, both in this example and the next, depends for its validity on a biblical cosmology. Consider four models. The first might be called the *open universe*.

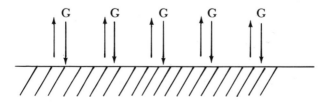

In this model, the Gs represent gods; the bottom of the diagram is the physical universe as it may be perceived by primitive peoples. My sister lived for years among the people of a certain New Guinea highland tribe. This tribe was pre-Stone Age in its technology—that is to say, however sophisiticated they were in other areas, their arrowheads were made of teak or bamboo, not stone (much less metal!). Their cosmology was much like the above model. They thought their activity affected the gods in some way; and these gods or, better, spirits (a more appropriate term, since the people were animists) in turn affected things, people, and events in the perceived world. Such spirits are somewhat whimsical and capricious; and so a great deal of time and care go into placating them and winning their favor. Right religious practice, avoidance of taboos, and the appropriate propitiating sacrifices, all help to ensure good crops, victory in the impending skirmish with the next tribe, the survival of the newborn baby, and the like. In this open universe, of course, science (as we think of it) is inconceivable. The gods (spirits) are too unpredictable; "laws" of cause and effect could not be discovered because they are unexpected, and, if they were somehow unearthed, they would be otherwise interpreted.

The second cosmology is the *closed universe*. It might be schematized like this:

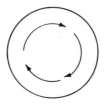

Everything that is, lies within the circle. And everything that takes place is to be explained by what is already in the circle. The best modern representative of this model of cosmology is science of a purely mechanistic and atheistic variety. There is nothing other than matter, energy, and space. Even time and chance are secondary. And every thing, every person, every event, every emotion, is to be explained by mechanistic principles of cause and effect. Science is not only possible; it is the only perspective considered legitimate.

Some might make an alteration to this model:

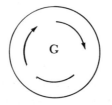

At first sight, this is quite an improvement: God is at the center of things. In fact, however, it differs little from the second model, because God is merely part of the mechanism. The best contemporary examples of this sort of cosmology are found among certain philosophers and theologians. These men are not atheists in the sense that they deny the existence of a god; but they are atheists in the sense that they deny that there is a personal and transcendent God. God becomes to them the ground of being, the impersonal force which directs man to authentic existence, and the like. God-words are common; but they refer to some "Being" far removed from the God portrayed in the Bible. And in terms of the way men see reality, science (and its laws of cause and effect) is the dominant force. Men may be called upon to make decisions, but sober reflection reveals that even such decisions are determined by the facts of science (either absolutely or according to the vagaries of statistical accident). I think this cosmology might be labeled the *quasi-theistic existentialist universe.*

A fourth model may be used to picture biblical cosmology. It is *the controlled universe.*

G

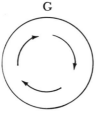

In this diagram, everything in the phenomenal universe is found, without exception, within the circle, along with every other created thing or being. Within this universe there are scientific laws to be discovered, and a patterned order which supports principles of cause and effect. Above this universe stands God. Actually, because of God's omnipresence, he stands both above this universe and in it (to use spatial categories). However, the infinite-personal God cannot be identified with his creation. In this sense, God stands ontologically over against his creation as its Creator and Sustainer. Designed by him, the universe hums along according to regular and predictable laws; but it does so only because he constantly exercises his sovereignty over the whole. No part of the system ever operates completely independently.

Moreover, at any instant he chooses, he is free to suspend or abolish scientific "laws"; that alone will account for such a miracle as the resurrection of Jesus from the dead. Man can discover scientific "laws"; indeed, he must, he is commissioned to do so as the steward of the creation. But the scientist who has adopted this biblical cosmology will not only recognize such laws and allow for divinely initiated exceptions, he will realize that those laws continue faithfully because of God's sustaining power. More specifically, since divine sovereignty is mediated through the Son, the Christian will hold that it is the Son who is, even now, "sustaining all things by his powerful word" (Heb. 1:3).

This biblical cosmology must be carefully distinguished from two counterfeits. The first is offered by Deism: God has started the whole machine running, like a giant watch; but he has now more or less left it to its own devices. The Bible pictures God, rather, as Sustainer. The second counterfeit recognizes God's sovereignty and transcendence, but pictures divine control as so immediate that science is excluded. The model becomes akin to the open universe I mentioned first, with all the Gs coalescing into one God. But this ill accounts for the orderliness and structure God has built into the system, and for the mandate he has given man concerning it.

Old Testament believers were quite aware that water evaporates, forms clouds which drop their rain, which provides rivulets, streams, and rivers which run to the sea; but more customarily they preferred to speak of God sending the rain. Such is the biblical cosmology.

This cosmology stands behind Matthew 6:26. Only those who have adopted such a cosmology will sense the thrust of the passage. The Christian looks at a beautifully plumed bird, or an eagle in flight, or a robin straining valiantly in a tug-of-war against a fat worm, and sees his Father's design and his Father's care. A bat swoops low at dusk; and the Christian does not say, "Ha! Marvelous aerodynamics, there! Evolution is quite remarkable." Rather, ornithologist or no, he testifies to God's activity behind the flight. And the wren who works all day to feed her chicks is evidence of God's provision for tiny baby birds. The believer who has understood and adopted this biblical cosmology has a constant, abundant array of evidence around him concerning divine providence and beneficence.

Jesus adds one more emphasis to this example. He asks, "Who of you by worrying can add a single hour to his life?" (6:27). This verse has been translated in many different ways. For example, in addition to the rendition of the NIV just given, we find:

Which of you by taking thought can add one cubit unto his stature? (KJV).

Can any of you, however much he worries, make himself an inch taller? (Phillips).

And which of you by being anxious can add one cubit to his span of life? (RSV).

Is there a man of you who by anxious thought can add a foot to his height? (NEB).

The problem is that the word translated "life" by the NIV can either mean stature or age. Zacchaeus was little in *stature* (Luke 19:3); Abraham was past the *age* to father children (Heb. 11:11). In the Greek New Testament, the same word is used in both verses. So in Matthew 6:27, we are asked which of us can add a single cubit (a linear measure of perhaps eighteen inches) to his stature or to his age. The latter seems inappropriate: linear measure can scarcely be added to age. But stature seems no more appropriate, because the force of the question in this case would depend on a very short linear measure, certainly not a cubit. All of the above efforts at translation have been generated by these difficulties.

I am inclined to follow those who see an idiom here, something like this: "Who of you by worrying can add to the pathway of his life a single cubit?" In America a person might say on his birthday, "Well, I've reached another milestone." Of course, he hasn't; what he has done is used linear measure as a metaphor for age. As a person walks the pathway of life, the time comes when God determines it will end. Worrying will not change that decree; he cannot travel a single cubit farther. So why worry about it?

Body and Clothes, 6:28–30

Clothes are scarcely less important than food; and Jesus treats both in the same way. "And why do you worry about clothes? See how the lilies of the field grow. They do not labor or spin. Yet I tell you that not even Solomon in all his splendor was dressed like one of these. If that is how God clothes the grass of the field, which is here today and tomorrow is thrown into the fire, will he not much more clothe you, O you of little faith?" (6:28-30). The word rendered lilies is, in the original, an obscure word which probably means "wild flowers," flowers of the field, complementing the "birds of the air" in verse 26.

Watch those flowers grow: they do not work to earn or buy their beauty. They grow. Each flower individually, and all of them in a field as they collectively decorate the green grass, make the opulent splendor of Solomon's clothing pall by comparison. This is God's work; the biblical cosmology is again presupposed. The Christian sees the fresh greenness of well-watered grass, and, whether or not he acknowledges the effect of chlorophyll, he certainly acknowledges the God behind the chlorophyll. God clothes the grass with spectacular arrays of flowers, even though the grass is destined to be mowed down and burned up. Shall he not be even more concerned to clothe us, his children?

In other words, biblical cosmology plus observant eyes engender real trust in God. Small wonder Jesus calls those who do not perceive these lessons, "men of little faith" (6:30).

Distinctive living, 6:31f.

At the end of Matthew 5, Jesus insists that his followers must love their enemies, for even pagans and public sinners love their friends. The norms of the kingdom require that our lifestyle be distinctive. Now in chapter 6 we discover—as in love, so also in freedom from worry: "So do not worry, saying, 'What shall we eat?' or 'What shall we drink?' or 'What shall we wear?' For the pagans run after all these things, and your heavenly Father knows that you need them" (6:31f.).

Lack of uncompromising trust in God is not only an affront to him, but also essentially pagan. In other words, verse 32 provides two important reasons why we are not to sound worried and frustrated like secular men. The first is that if we worry as pagans do, it is transparent that we are pursuing the same things they are; but if we are, then because the kingdom values are so different, the kingdom is necessarily being denied. Second, such worry on the part of those who profess faith in God constitutes some sort of denial of that profession, since the heavenly Father is well aware of our needs (cf. also 6:8), and our conduct is advertising loudly that we don't believe it.

Our worries must not sound like the worries of the world. When the Christian faces the pressure of examinations, does he sound like the pagan in the next room? When he is short of money, even for the essentials, does he complain with the same tone, the same words, the same attitude, as those around him? Away with secular thinking. The follower of Jesus will be concerned to have a distinctive lifestyle, one that is characterized by values and perspectives so un-pagan that his life and conduct are, as it were, stamped all over with the words, "Made in the kingdom of God."

What does this principle imply for Christians in the professions, in trade unions, in big business? Suppose even one tenth of contemporary nominal evangelicals pored over the pages of Scripture to establish what their lifestyles should be like, and, with balance, determination, meekness, and courage, found grace to live accordingly. What transformation would be effected in our world! How the light would alleviate the darkness; how the salt would preserve society!

In the fourth century, the Roman Emperor Julian the Apostate, failed in his efforts to suppress Christianity, largely because of the distinctive living he found among believers. He told his officials, "We ought to be ashamed. Not a beggar is to be found among the Jews, and those godless Galileans [he meant the Christians] feed not only their own people but ours as well, whereas our people receive no assistance whatever from us." We have some things to learn from the early Christians (not to mention many later ones, such as the Anabaptists) about the sharing of material things; but, more broadly, we have even more things to learn about the importance of the kind of living which is eager to pursue kingdom perspectives.

The question immediately at hand is worry. Would it not be wonderful if some world leader were forced to say today, "We ought to be ashamed. Not a worrier is to be found among those fanatics who call themselves Christians. They cope not only with the pressures faced by other men, but the pressures we put on them as well. And then they go and give comfort to some of us when we worry, whereas our people are constantly gulping down tranquilizers, visiting assorted counselors and mass-producing overweight ulcers."

The heart of the matter, 6:33

Because our heavenly Father knows what we need and has committed himself to be gracious to his children, Jesus gives this pledge: "But seek first his kingdom and his righteousness, and all these things will be given to you as well" (6:33). Our part is to avoid consuming worry, even over essentials, and to pursue the kingdom of God. The word "seek" here is present imperative, suggesting unceasing quest. God's part is then to provide his children with what they need.

Three limitations must be observed. (1) This promise is to the children of God, not to all men indiscriminately. This is made clear by the contrast between Jesus' disciples and pagans in 6:31f., as well as by the condition in 6:33a itself: Seek first his kingdom and his righteousness. (2) Jesus promises that necessities will be provided (in context, food, drink, and clothes are specified), not luxuries. Many Christians in the West would think it very hard indeed if they had to live at subsistence level, for they have long since come to take as necessities things which others would assess as luxuries. God in his lavish mercy often gives much more than the essentials; but he here pledges himself only to the latter. (3) I think the major exception to this pledge occurs when Christians are suffering for righteousness' sake. Some are martyred by starvation and by exposure. The overwhelming importance of the kingdom may require self-sacrifice even to this ultimate degree.

God does keep this promise. In the affluent West, too few of us, especially if we are young, have experienced his faithfulness in this regard. But some have been privileged to experience pressure to the point where they have had absolutely no recourse but God. I know a couple who, some years ago, were serving a small, lower class church in Montreal. On Christmas Day, the man distributed food packages, gathered by the church, to the destitute in the vicinity. He returned home to his wife, and both of them thanked the Lord for the food with which he had provided them—one can of beans. One half hour later they were invited out to a Christmas dinner.

Such stories could be multiplied endlessly. God answers prayer and supplies the needs of his own. To this I testify from many experiences of his grace, especially during the long years while I was a student, frequently without any money at all.

But at least I *was* a student. What shall we say of the desperate hunger that stalks so much of the globe today? I have seen little of it; but what I have seen of it in a Christian context confirms the promise of Matthew 6:33. God provides for his own. This *in no way* reduces our responsibility to share what we have; rather, it enhances it, for God's most common way of meeting the material needs of his poor children is by laying such needs on the hearts and consciences of others among his children.

This prompts two other reflections which, even if they are not explicitly stated in the text itself, are quite important. They speak to questions lurking in the back of our minds in these days when evangelicals are reassessing their social responsibility, and at the same time the so-called "Protestant work ethic" has come under attack.

On the first point, we Christians desperately need to assess our goals and commitments in the light of what the Scriptures teach about caring for the hungry (see Prov. 22:9; 25:21f.; Isa. 32:6; 58:6ff.; Ezek. 16:49; 18:7; Matt. 25:42; Luke 3:11; 12:48; Acts 4:32ff.). Christians first of all ought to support their own, but they must reach out to others as well. Sooner or later the mad race toward more and more possessions must cease: let Christians choose to get out of the race now, before there is no choice.

On the second point, work and profit are not to be despised. The Puritans receive much bad popular press; but they have a great deal to teach us about working with integrity. They saw their work as a form of service to the Lord, and, believing that they should be faithful in small things as in great, worked with zealous industry. Moreover, their desire for education brought them advancement, and their simple lifestyle multiplied their savings. (How much does an "average" family of four spend *per annum* on cigarettes, junk and excess food, alcohol, and questionable entertainment? This arithmetical exercise produces staggering results.) The tragedy of the Puritans was that later generations came to believe, though few would be so crass as to express it, that righteousness and industry were worthwhile virtues *because* they led to thrift and wealth. They disciplined themselves *so that* they might accumulate things. Gradually a biblical perspective was subverted into an abhorrent materialism.

Disciples of Jesus must think clearly about these things. They will seek first their Father's kingdom and righteousness, assured that he will provide enough to cover their needs. And, industrious and honest as they may be, they will refuse to tie their lives and happiness to treasures which can be corrupted and stolen. And rich or poor, they will struggle to understand how best to please their Father by using the wealth he has entrusted to them.

The goal, then, is always the kingdom of God. For the Christian, the disciple of Jesus, there is no other. The logic entailed by this simple fact orients his thinking to kingdom values and concomitantly abolishes worry over merely temporal things, a worry which compromises his trust in his heavenly Father.

Final reason for reducing worry, 6:34

I think Jesus must have said the words in Matthew 6:34 with a wry smile. So far his reasons for sending worry to oblivion have been essentially theological. They have turned on the compassion and providence of God, and on the superlative value of the kingdom. But this last reason is purely pragmatic: "Therefore do not worry about tomorrow, for tomorrow will worry about itself. Each day has enough trouble of its own" (6:34).

It is as if Jesus recognizes that there will be some unavoidable worry today after all. But let's limit it to the concerns of today! Our gracious God intends us to take one step at a time, no more; to be responsible today and not fret about tomorrow. "Each day has enough trouble of its own." And if there will be new troubles tomorrow, so also will there be fresh grace.

✿   ✿   ✿

The person who enters the kingdom adopts the perspectives of the kingdom. In broadest terms, this entails unswerving loyalty to the values dictated by God, and uncompromised trust in God. In the light of so high a calling, our self-examination will produce some bleak results; and we shall want to pray the words of T. B. Pollock (1836-1896):

> We have not known Thee as we ought,
> Nor learned Thy wisdom, grace, and power;
> The things of earth have filled our thought,
> And trifles of the passing hour.
> Lord, give us light Thy truth to see,
> And make us wise in knowing Thee.

We have not feared Thee as we ought,
Nor bowed beneath Thine aweful eye,
Nor guarded deed, and word, and thought,
Rememb'ring that our God was nigh.
Lord, give us faith to know Thee near,
And grant the grace of holy fear.

We have not loved Thee as we ought,
Nor cared that we are loved by Thee;
Thy presence we have coldly sought,
And feebly longed Thy face to see.
Lord, give a pure and loving heart
To feel and own the love Thou art.

We have not served Thee as we ought;
Alas, the duties left undone,
The work with little fervor wrought,
The battles lost or scarcely won!
Lord, give the zeal, and give the might,
For Thee to toil, for Thee to fight.

When shall we know Thee as we ought,
And fear, and love, and serve aright?
When shall we, out of trial brought,
Be perfect in the land of light?
Lord, may we day by day prepare
To see Thy face, and serve Thee there.

5 *MATTHEW 7:1-12*

BALANCE AND PERFECTION

We human beings display a vast capacity for self-deception. For example, we prostitute righteousness into self-righteousness, and perfection into a perfect reputation; but we accomplish this prostitution so cleverly that we are at best only vaguely aware of the monstrosity we have wrought. Against all such aped religion Jesus has already spoken trenchantly (Matt. 6:1-18), filling out the warning with searching counter-demands which require heart-adherence to kingdom perspectives (Matt 6:19-34).

Before Jesus winds up the Sermon on the Mount and drives home the alternatives which men must face (Matt. 7:13-27), he warns against three other dangers. The first two are cast in negative terms—we are not to be judgmental (7:1-5) and yet we are not to be undiscriminating (7:6). The third is formulated positively: We must persist in our pursuit of God, exercising childlike trust as we do so (7:7-11). By looking closely at these three warnings, we shall discover how they build toward the golden rule (7:12).

THE DANGER OF BEING JUDGMENTAL
Matthew 7:1-5

The principle, 7:1

It is easy to see how powerful and dangerous the temptation to be judgmental can be. The challenge to be holy has been taken seriously, and a fair degree of discipline, service and formal obedience have been painstakingly won. Now, I tell myself, I can afford to look down my long nose at my less disciplined peers and colleagues. Or perhaps I have actually experienced a generous measure of God's grace, but somehow I have misconstrued it and come to think that I have earned it. As a result I may look askance at those whose vision, in my view, is not as large as my own; whose faith is not as stable; whose grasp of the deep truths of God not as masterful; whose service record is not as impressive (in men's eyes, at least); whose efforts have not been as substantial. These people are diminished in my eyes; I consider their value as people inferior to my own value.

The harping, critical attitude may become so poisonous that men whose spiritual stature, personal integrity, and useful service are all vastly superior to my own, somehow emerge as spiritual pygmies and intellectual paupers by the time I have finished my assessment. Perhaps some small deficiency or inconsistency in their lives has, in my view, utterly vitiated their stature. If in Matthew 6 love of money and distrustful anxiety ruin Christian character, in Matthew 7 the same result is achieved by this scurrilous sort of zeal.

All this, of course, is a form of raw hypocrisy (see 7:5), the second of the three forms of hypocrisy I mentioned earlier (see p. 57). Lest the challenges and impeccable standards of the Sermon on the Mount evoke such ugly sin, Jesus warns, "Do not judge, or you too will be judged" (7:1).

We will be wise to consider first what this text does *not* say. It certainly does not command the sons of God, the disciples of Jesus, to be amorphous, undiscerning blobs who never under any circumstance whatsoever hold any opinions about right and wrong. Are we to say nothing about the rights and wrongs of a Hitler, a Stalin, a Nixon? of adultery, economic exploitation, laziness, deceit? The New Testament itself excludes such a fatuous interpretation. A few verses on, the Lord Jesus himself alludes to certain people as pigs and dogs (7:6)—some sort of negative judgment has certainly taken place! A little further on, Jesus warns, "Watch out for false prophets. They came to you in sheep's clothing, but inwardly they are ferocious wolves" (7:15). By these words Jesus not only labels certain teachers with the most damning epithets, but demands that his followers recognize such teachers for what they are; and that is certainly an exercise which requires the use of discriminating faculties.

Elsewhere, the apostle Paul is prepared to hand over a certain promiscuous man to Satan (I Cor. 5:5), demanding that his local church discipline him; such discipline requires judgment. In Galatians 1:8f. Paul calls down an anathema on all who preach some version of the gospel other than the true gospel which Paul himself preaches. In Philipians 3:2 he uses strong language to warn his readers against certain false teachers: "Watch out for those dogs, those men who do evil, those mutilators of the flesh." And this language is mild compared with that in Galatians 5:12. John likewise demands some kind of judgment when he writes, "Dear friends, do not believe every spirit, but test the spirits to see whether they are from God, because many false prophets have gone out into the world" (I John 4:1). Moreover, when a crowd misjudges Jesus because his healing ministry extends to the Sabbath, he does not forbid all judgment, but replies rather, "Stop judging by mere appearances, and make a right judgment" (John 7:24).

What then does Jesus mean by his imperative in Matthew 7:1, "Do not judge, or you too will be judged"? Much of the confusion here is resolved when the semantic range of the Greek word translated "judge" is understood. "To judge" can mean to discern, to judge judicially, to be judgmental, to condemn (judicially or otherwise). The context must determine the precise shade of meaning. The context here argues that the verse means, "Do not be judgmental." Do not adopt a critical spirit, a condemning attitude. The same verb is found twice, with identical meaning, in Romans 14:10ff: "You, then, why do you *judge* your brother? Or why do you look down on your brother? For we will all stand before God's judgment seat. It is written: 'As I live,' says the Lord, 'every knee will bow before me; every tongue will confess to God.' So then, each of us will give an account of himself to God. Therefore, let us stop *passing judgment* on one another. Instead, make up your mind not to put any stumbling block or obstacle in your brother's way." Jesus himself commands, "Do not be judgmental."

This is not an easy area of one's life to sort out. On the one hand, some people are so critical that they feast on roast preacher every Sunday lunch; and some preachers are so critical they level verbal barrages at most of their colleagues, especially those more fruitful than they. On the other hand, Jesus' disciples ought to recognize some preachers as false because of their fruit (7:16), and dismiss them accordingly; the preacher who credits all his peers with precisely the same grace and insight falls far below Paul's discriminating attitudes. The problem is that the Christian's responsibility to discern, once granted, is readily warped into justification for harping criticism. The arch-critic is thoroughly at home with all the passages which encourage us to spot false prophets by their fruit. "I'm not being judgmental," he protests, "I'm just a fruit inspector." But by his own mouth, he stands condemned; he has become a fruit *inspector*, he has taken on himself some special role.

What is fundamentally at stake, I think, is attitude. This is clearly seen in that particular kind of critical spirit found in the gossip. It is not always the case that what the gossip says is malicious; what he says might, in fact, be strictly true. But it is always the case that he says it maliciously; that is, he speaks without any desire to build up, or any real concern to instill discernment. He wants only to puff himself up, or to be heard, or to enhance his own reputation, or to demean the person about whom he is speaking.

If a Christian's *attitude* is right, provision is made for him to face another brother with his fault (see Matt. 18:15ff.). Indeed, spiritual leaders will not ignore open sin in one of their Christian brothers, but will try and restore him—gently, and aware of their own weakness (Gal. 6:1).

"Do not be judgmental," Jesus says, and then adds, "or you too will be judged" (7:1). The latter clause may perhaps be taken like the first: if you are judgmental, others will be judgmental toward you. Alternatively, depending on the ambiguity of the Greek verb, the sentence may mean: do not be judgmental, or you will be condemned (whether by God or others). Either way, the clause adds stinging pungency to the injunction, and introduces the theological justification for abolishing all judgmental attitudes.

The theological justification, 7:2

"For in the same way you judge others, you will be judged, and with the measure you use, it will be measured to you" (7:2). It is theoretically possible to understand these words, like the words of 7:1b, in more than one way. They may mean that the measure we use on others will be the measure others use on us; the person with a critical spirit is inviting a lot of criticism. Alternatively, verse 2 may mean that the measure we use on others will be the measure God himself will use on us.

I think it is the latter meaning that is in view; and if so, the ambiguity in 7:1b must be interpreted in a similar way. The point of these two verses is not that we should be moderate in our judging in order that others will be moderate toward us, but rather that we should abolish judgmental attitudes lest we ourselves stand utterly condemned before God. A judgmental attitude excludes us from God's pardon, for it betrays an unbroken spirit. The thought is akin to 5:7 and 6:14f.: "Blessed are the merciful, for they will be shown mercy. . . . For if you forgive men when they sin against you, your heavenly Father will also forgive you. But if you do not forgive men their sins, your Father will not forgive your sins." For in the same way you judge others, you will be judged. . . .

Some rabbis said that God had two measures by which he assessed men, the measure of justice and the measure of mercy. It may be that Jesus in 7:2 is using this belief to drive home his point—the measure we use, of these two, will be applied to us. For example, suppose we come across a wretched liar. How do we look upon him? If we measure him by justice alone, we will be very critical and condemning. But that measure will then be turned on us: How truthful are we? How often do we slant reports and stories to make a point or earn favor? Or perhaps we apply the standard of justice to the adulterer or prostitute. How will we fare when the same standard is applied to us, especially in the light of Matthew 5:27-30? Or again, perhaps we apply God's standard of justice to wealthy men who exploit the poor by unfair practices and greed. But how often have we been greedy? How often have we robbed others of value for money (even, for example, in our work)? Do we really want the standard of God's justice to be applied to ourselves in the way we are prone to apply it to others?

As we have seen, this does not mean that the disciple of Jesus must never speak against any sin, exercising a sort of insipid, overlooking mercy. God's standard of justice will not go away. These verses attack judgmental attitudes, but they do not deny that real sins may well be present. In the example which follows (7:3-5), the speck of sawdust in the patient's eye does in fact require removal, even if the operation should not be performed by a surgeon with a plank in his own eye.

Moreover, this passage does not suggest that we can earn God's mercy by exercising a little mercy ourselves. Mercy by definition cannot be earned. But we may exclude ourselves from mercy by sustained haughtiness and arrogance, by an attitude which reflects the antithesis of true poverty of spirit. God, in fact, exercises both justice and mercy, even toward his own people (of this I shall say more at the beginning of the next chapter). Therefore his people must reflect God's character by living justly and showing mercy. And because they are conscious of their own shortcomings and rebellion, they cannot but be profoundly grateful for mercy they have experienced even while they strive for perfection and magnify holiness. This balanced perspective keeps them both from a judgmental spirit and from moral apathy.

Perhaps I should say in passing that some people relate 7:1f. to the "Golden Rule" in 7:12. They feel this is strong evidence that 7:2 has to do with the way men will judge us, not at all with the way God will judge us. They understand 7:1f. to mean that one important reason we should not be judgmental to others is so that as a result others will not be judgmental toward us; this, they say, is one aspect of the "Golden Rule." For reasons I have already given, I think such an interpretation fails to comprehend 7:1f.; but I hasten to add that it equally fails to understand the "Golden Rule" (7:12). This rule tells us to do to others what we would have them do to us; it does not tell us to do nice things to others *in order that* they might do nice things to us. Doing to others what we would have them do to us establishes a code for our own behavior; it does not establish a *reason* for that behavior. The reason is given in the next clause: such behavior sums up the Law and the Prophets.

An example, 7:3-5

"Why do you look at the speck of sawdust in your brother's eye and pay no attention to the plank in your own eye? How can you say to your brother, 'Let me take the speck out of your eye,' when all the time there is a plank in your own eye? You hypocrite, first take the plank out of your own eye, and then you will see clearly to remove the speck from your brother's eye" (7:3-5).

This colorful illustration must not be permitted to lose its power because of its familiarity, still less because it is set in the categories of ophthalmology. The situation depicted by this brief scenario occurs so frequently and so pathetically in professing Christian circles that the contrast between a speck of sawdust and a plank or log is not at all exaggerated.

The most obvious example in the Bible, I suppose, is found in II Samuel 12:1-7. King David steals another man's wife. Despite his large harem, he lusts after this particular woman, seduces her, and later discovers that she has become pregnant by him. Her husband is absent at the military front (fighting the king's wars) and so David arranges to have him killed. The king is now guilty of both adultery and murder. The prophet Nathan enters the royal court; but instead of confronting his monarch outright, he tells a parable, a short story about a poor farmer whose one little lamb has been stolen by a rich, powerful neighbor with a large flock of his own. David is incensed; perhaps some of the force of his wrath arises from his own suppressed guilt. In seething indignation, and quite unconscious of any irony, he asks who this wicked farmer is. Nathan replies, "You are the man."

Somehow, King David, incredibly blind, had been unconscious of the plank in his own eye as he fumed over the speck of sawdust in the rich farmer's eye.

It is terribly easy to imitate David's conduct, in one way or another. Sometimes we accomplish this by focusing on certain public sins which others are prone to commit, and denouncing those sins with gusto, while remaining disturbingly oblivious to the sins to which we ourselves are especially attracted. Doctrinal critics can be among the most offensive in this regard. The doctrinal critic may agree that another person is a brother in Christ, has been significantly used of the Lord, is thoughtful and sincere in his submission to Scripture; but because the critic focuses on the one area of doctrine in which the two disagree, this other brother may be painted publicly in hues of gray and black. That Christians are to demonstrate observable love (John 13:34f.; 17:20-23) is lost to view while the critic "defends the truth."

I am not minimizing the significance of truth, nor denying that there are limits to fellowship. I am saying two things. First, genuine believers have more in common than they recognize when, with a sectarian mentality, they focus attention and energy on points of difference, largely to reinforce what they construe as their own *raison d'être*. If I wholeheartedly embrace only those fellow Christians who see things exactly the way I do, I will never embrace anyone, except, perhaps, a handful of weak-minded followers. Second, we must never lose sight of the stress in Matthew 7:1-5 on attitudes. Christians will honestly disagree on doctrinal points, but to become very heated helps no one. There ought to be clear-headed discussion of the differences, with honest submission to the Word of God and a repudiation of arguments which consistently and without cause ascribe unworthy motives to the opposing brothers. Who knows? Perhaps frank discussion and humble examination both of the Scriptures and of the way the other man understands them will bring about consensus of opinion. At the very least it will produce an awareness of the dimensions of the debate, and establish the points where there is, at present, irreconcilable difference of opinion, some of which may be removed by further reflection and research.

Ironically, the worst fault-finder, whether in doctrinal or other realms, cannot be convinced of his fault. If the speck he has discovered in another person's eye is shown to be an illusion, or if the large log in his own eye is gently pointed out, he hunts and pecks until he finds another speck in his target's eye. This critic always looks for something else to criticize; he cannot feel he is sound unless he is constantly denouncing and condemning. I am not sure how he envisages his responsibility to love his neighbor as himself, nor what he thinks of the words, "Love is patient, love is kind. It does not envy, it is not proud. It is not rude, it is not self-seeking, it is not easily angered, it keeps no record of wrongs. Love does not delight in evil, but rejoices in the truth. It always protects, always trusts, always hopes, always perseveres. . . . The end of all things is near. Therefore be clear-minded and self-controlled so that you can pray. Above all, love each other deeply, because love covers over a multitude of sins" (I Cor. 13:4-7; I Peter. 4:7f.).

The more I reflect on this passage, the more I find I am self-condemned. God grant me grace to practice what I preach.

I used to think that those who most needed Matthew 7:1-5 were young people, especially students. They are struggling to establish their own identities, trying to come to terms with new ideas. These new ideas are quickly espoused and stoutly defended or as quickly rejected and unthinkingly mocked. But young people and students are far from being the only ones who go through periods of identity crisis and of critical exposure to new thinking. Older people, fearful of their positions, concerned with their prestige, and often disturbed by what they take to be the lack of productivity in their lives, often become singularly defensive, rigid, judgmental, intolerant, even nasty and petty. The young, at least, may grow out of it; but for the old to reject such a long-established pattern of behavior may take a dramatic display of divine intervention, perhaps in the form of a crushing, devastating experience that engenders humility.

The person who is scrupulously careful about removing the planks from his own eyes is not thereby absolved from all further responsibility. Having gained the ability to see clearly, he can help remove the speck from his brother's eye (7:5). Indeed, only then will his brother welcome his assistance.

THE DANGER OF BEING UNDISCRIMINATING
Matthew 7:6

We come now to what is essentially the converse danger to the one treated by our Lord in Matthew 7:1-5: the danger of being undiscriminating. It is easy to see how this new danger arises. The disciple of Jesus has been told to love his neighbor as himself, and to love his enemies. He is to mirror God's graciousness, the God who even-handedly sends his rain upon both the just and the unjust. He has just been told never to adopt a judgmental mentality. As a result, he is in chronic danger of becoming wishy-washy, of refusing legitimate distinctions between truth and error, good and evil. He may even try to treat all men in *exactly* the same way, succumbing to a remarkable lack of discrimination.

And so, after warning us against judgmentalism, Jesus warns us against being undiscriminating, especially in our choice of people to whom we present the wonderful riches of the gospel. However, in seeking to do full justice to this warning in 7:6, we ought not fail to note that five verses are reserved for judgmental people, and only one for undiscerning people. That ratio reflects an accurate assessment of where the greater danger lies.

The Lord Jesus says, "Do not give dogs what is sacred; do not throw your pearls to pigs. If you do, they may trample them under their feet, and then turn and tear you to pieces." The dogs in view are not cuddly pets with wagging tails and affectionate natures, friendly creatures that love to have their ears scratched. They are semi-wild hounds that roam the streets and hills, tongues hanging from their mouths and burrs clinging to their filthy coats as they forage for food in savage packs. And the

Palestinian domestic pig was not only an abomination to the Jew, but, most probably derived from the European wild boar, it was capable of certain violence. The two animals together serve as a model of people who are savage, vicious, held in abomination. These two are brought together again in II Peter 2:22, in an equally negative context: "Of them [certain people] the proverbs are true: 'A dog returns to its vomit,' and, 'A sow that is washed goes back to her wallowing in the mud.'"

Jesus sketches a picture of a man holding a bag of precious pearls, confronting a pack of hulking hounds and some wild pigs. As the animals glare hungrily, he takes out his pearls and sprinkles them on the street. Thinking they are about to gulp some bits of food, the animals pounce on the pearls. Swift disillusionment sets in—the pearls are too hard to chew, quite tasteless, and utterly unappetizing. Enraged, the wild animals spit out the pearls, turn on the man and tear him to pieces.

Camping can be enjoyed in vast wilderness areas of North America. But one of the rules to be observed unfailingly is, Don't feed the bears! Feed the ground squirrels, feed the deer, feed the racoons, even feed the coyotes; but don't feed the bears. If they aren't satisfied, they will turn and tear you to pieces.

In metaphorical language (which makes his warning even more shocking than if he had spoken without metaphor), Jesus is commanding his disciples not to share the richest parts of spiritual truth with persons who are persistently vicious, irresponsible, and unappreciative. Just as the pearls were unappreciated by the savage animals, but only enraged them and made them dangerous, so also many of the riches of God's revelation are unappreciated by many people. And, painful as it is to see it, these rich truths may only serve to enrage them.

In the New Testament, there are several examples of this principle in action. In Matthew 15:14, Jesus, speaking of certain Pharisees, tells his disciples, "Leave them; they are blind guides. If a blind man leads a blind man, both will fall into a pit." According to Acts 18:5f., Paul abandons his ministry to the Jews in Corinth because they oppose him and become abusive. Instead he turns to the Gentiles to minister to them. Paul recommends a similar course of action to Titus concerning divisive people within the professing Christian community: "Warn a divisive person once, and then warn him a second time. After that have nothing to do with him. You may be sure that such a man is warped and sinful; he is self-condemned" (Titus 3:10f.).

I would like to draw attention to five implications or allusions embedded in this pithy injunction. First, it is no accident that Jesus speaks of pearls, and not gravel. The man in the scenario is in possession of great wealth. Interpreting the metaphor, we learn that the good news of Jesus Christ, with all of history and revelation pointing toward it, really is a priceless treasure. It is wonderful beyond words. All physical wealth palls to insignificance beside it. Because this is God's world, nothing is more important to me than to have my sins forgiven and to be accepted by him; and nothing is more wonderful than the way God has accomplished this by sending his own son to die in my behalf. God has graciously given to men, both in human language (the Bible) and in a human person (Jesus), true and sure revelation of himself; and nothing, absolutely nothing, is richer or more important or of more consequence than that.

Second, however, is the somber recognition that not all men will receive this revelation. Some, like dogs and pigs confronting pearls, remain utterly insensitive to this revelation. It does not gratify their immediate appetites, and they have no other criteria by which to assess it. Thus, by these verses we are being prepared for the division of the human race into two groups, portrayed by the Lord Jesus in Matthew 7:13ff.

Third, it is not simply that some do not receive this revelation. For the chief thrust of 7:6 is that Jesus' disciples are not even to present the riches of that revelation to certain people of vicious and unappreciative disposition. Their cynical mockery, their intellectual arrogance, their love of moral decay, and their vaunted self-sufficiency make them utterly impervious to the person and words of Christ. Over the years I have gradually come to the place where I refuse to attempt to explain Christianity and introduce Christ to the person who just wants to mock and argue and ridicule. It accomplishes nothing good, and there are so many other opportunities where time and energy can be invested more profitably.

This unavoidable conclusion must be balanced with a fourth observation, that this injunction from the Lord Jesus himself is set in a broader context, which demands love for enemies and a quality of life characterized by perfect righteousness. In other words, the fact that Christians ought not throw their pearls to dogs and pigs does not give them a license to be nasty and vindictive, still less to ignore all else that Jesus has taught. Moreover, there is no justification in this verse for neglecting all verbal witness on the grounds that there are only dogs and pigs out there who are, without exception, vicious. Many—if not most—thinking adults who have become sincere disciples of the Lord Jesus Christ begin this pilgrimage by balking, and not a few begin by mocking.

There are many situations in which Christians need to persist in their witness and be patient with their sowing of God's truth. The harvest will come in due time if we do not faint from cowardice or laziness first. What Jesus is calling for is discernment; and the essence of discernment is knowing that simple rules cannot be expected to crank out an infallible answer. Here, again, we do well to try to follow the example of the Teacher himself. It is eminently profitable to examine his approach to different individuals and groups. He can dismiss a group (as we have seen him do, in Matt. 15:14), write off a Herod (Luke 13:31-33), promise judgment to whole cities (Matt. 11:20-24); but he can be patient with a group (see Luke 9:51-55; Mark 6:31-34), offer indisputable evidence to a doubting Thomas (John 20:24ff.), and weep over a city (Luke 19:41ff.). Christians dare not decide which side of Jesus' reactions they will follow most closely; they must follow both. And I suspect that the stronger the inclination to follow one side at the expense of the other, the greater the danger of imbalance, and the stronger the need to grow in discernment and conformity to Christ.

Moreover, although Christians must learn discretion and spiritual discernment, and therefore refrain from throwing around their pearls with reckless abandon, nevertheless the bearing and quality of their life may conceivably be used of God to prompt the dogs and pigs to reflect. If there is hope for lost and hardened people, it lies, as James Montgomery Boice has said, "in the sovereignty of God and in the demonstrable reality of true Christian living." While writing these lines I was called aside to explain the fundamentals of biblical Christianity to a medical student from one of the universities nearby. It is worth noting that, according to him, his first attraction to the Bible and to Christ was prompted in part by intellectual curiosity, but more particularly by the quality of life of some Christian students he has known. The salt had not lost its savor; the light was still shining.

In sum, we are to be careful in our handling of the truths of biblical revelation, for they are holy things, and must not be thrown around indiscriminately, but thoughtfully, carefully, responsibly, strategically. And, it is probably valid to deduce that the discrimination explicitly required by this text constitutes only a part of the larger responsibility to be discriminating.

THE DANGER OF LACKING A TRUSTING PERSISTENCE
Matthew 7:7-11

It is painfully easy to understand how those who lack persistence in the Christian faith develop. Someone gets all excited about the teaching of Jesus. So many things attract him: the noble sentiments, the call to self-sacrifice, the sublime moral tone, the uncompromised purity, the emphasis on untarnished truth, the farsighted faith, the winsome freedom from a judgmental mentality—splendid stuff! And in committing himself to this fine teaching he experiences a sort of catharsis which he takes to be a sign of spiritual life. Thus encouraged, he spurts ahead, his behavior promising a rich harvest of spiritual graces. No one is more eager to volunteer for spiritual work, no one more faithful in attendance at Bible studies and prayer meetings, no one more concerned to follow Christ's teachings in all spheres of human existence.

And then he fizzles, ignominiously flickers once or twice, and sputters out. It is as if he bloomed in some rocky place without much depth of earth. The seed of truth falls into this soil, and grows up quickly for no other reason than that the soil is so shallow. But when the full heat of the summer sun pelts down its searing rays, the plant's young roots have nowhere to go for moisture. The plant is scorched, and it withers and dies. In Jesus' words, "What was sown on rocky places is the man who hears the word and at once receives it with joy. But since he has no root, he lasts only a short time. When trouble or persecution comes because of the word, he quickly falls away" (Matt. 13:20f.; cf. 13:1-9).

What has gone wrong with this person? First, he lacks persistence, he is short on sticking power. True Christian commitment perseveres. "No one who puts his hand to the plow and looks back is fit for service in the kingdom of God" (Luke 9:62), Jesus insists—an attitude reflected equally in John, who says that those who draw back have never really belonged to Christ's people (I John 2:19). But second, and more important, this flash-in-the-pan disciple has been motivated by high sentiment and noble thought, and has somehow entirely missed the significance of the first beatitude: "Blessed are the poor in spirit, for theirs is the kingdom of heaven" (5:3). He is riding on his determination, his own recently stimulated lofty ideals. Incredibly, the Sermon on the Mount makes him think he can live by its precepts all by himself. Instead of seeing his own spiritual bankruptcy by the light of the Sermon on the Mount, he sees only the beauty of the light itself; and therefore instead of turning to God and asking for the grace, mercy, forgiveness, acceptance, and help which his spiritually bankrupt state requires, he merely turns over a new leaf. Small wonder he is soon discouraged and defeated.

That is why Jesus says, "Ask and it shall be given you; seek and you will find; knock and the door will be opened to you. For everyone who asks receives; he who seeks finds; and to him who knocks, the door will be opened" (7:7f.). In the perfect three-fold symmetry of these two verses, the imperatives are emphatic and in the present tense. Keep on asking, keep on seeking, keep on knocking; ask, seek, knock, and keep on doing it; for "everyone who asks receives; he who sees finds; and to him who knocks the door will be opened."

Persistence is required. But persistence in what? The answer is persistence in prayer—not prayer envisaged as an occasional pious request for some isolated blessing, but, in the context of the Sermon on the Mount, prayer that is a burning pursuit of God. This asking is an asking for the virtues Jesus has just expounded; this seeking is a seeking for God; this knocking is a knocking at heaven's throne room. It is a divinely empowered response to God's open invitation: "You will seek me and you will find me when you search for me with all your heart" (Jer. 29:13).

The kingdom of heaven requires poverty of spirit, purity of heart, truth, compassion, a non-retaliatory spirit, a life of integrity; and we lack all of these things. Then let us ask for them! Are you as holy, as meek, as truthful, as loving, as pure, as obedient to God as you would like to be? Then ask him for grace that these virtues may multiply in your life! Such asking, when sincere and humble, is already a step of repentance and faith, for it is an acknowledgement that the virtues the kingdom requires you do not possess, and that these same virtues only God can give. Moreover, I suspect that this asking, seeking, and knocking has a total package as its proper object. It does not seek holiness but spurn obedience; it does not seek obedience but hedge when it comes to purity. It is a wholehearted pursuit of the kingdom of God and his righteousness. And this pursuit is stamped by stamina: it is a *persistent* asking, seeking, knocking (cf. also Luke 11:5-10; 18:1-8; I Thess. 5:17).

The Western world is not characterized by prayer. By and large, to our unspeakable shame, even genuine Christians in the West are not characterized by prayer. Our environment loves hustle and bustle, smooth organization and powerful institutions, human self-confidence and human achievement, new opinions and novel schemes; and the church of Jesus Christ has conformed so thoroughly to this environment that it is often difficult to see how it differs in these matters from contemporary paganism. There are, of course, exceptions; but I am referring to what is characteristic. Our low spiritual ebb is directly traceable to the flickering feebleness of our prayers: "You do not have, because you do not ask God. When you ask, you do not receive, because you ask with wrong motives, that you may spend what you get on your pleasures" (James 4:2b-3).

There is an unavoidable correlative to this asking. It follows inescapably that if we must ask, we cannot receive the virtues characteristic of those in the kingdom unless they are given by God. This observation is of extreme importance because it forms part of a motif which flows through the entire New Testament. To put it another way, no one earns his place in the kingdom of God. No one chalks up merit points until he has accumulated enough to inherit eternal life. No one is capable, by himself, of even approaching the quality of life characterized by the Sermon on the Mount. And certainly no one will ever enter the consummated kingdom simply because he has determined to improve himself and make himself presentable before God.

The first beatitude has already set the tone: God's approval rests on the person who is poor in spirit. Such a person, recognizing his personal spiritual bankruptcy and his personal inability to conform to kingdom perspectives, will be eager to ask God for grace and help, impatient to seek the blessings only God can give, delighted to knock at the portals of heaven. He also recognizes that salvation now—and the full richness of that salvation in the consummated kingdom—depends on God's grace, God's free unmerited favor. This man rejoices to read Jesus' invitation to ask, seek, and knock. He comes as a humble petitioner, seeking pardon and grace.

It becomes clear, then, how Jesus' words serve as an antidote to the danger of withering in rocky soil. The person who becomes all excited about the lofty ideals of the Sermon on the Mount must learn that no spiritual progress is made apart from God's grace; then he will understand that there is nothing more crucial than to ask God for that grace. Moreover, he will begin to grasp the solemn fact that biblical Christianity is not some temporary high to be assumed or discarded at will according to the present level of excitement or discouragement. Rather, it is an orientation of the whole life, an eternal commitment that depends for its success on the trustworthiness of God. Failures and setbacks there may be; but God remains utterly faithful and free from partiality and the vagaries of human whims, and still gives to the one who asks, presents spiritual treasure to the one who seeks, and opens to the one who knocks.

Does God do this begrudgingly? This is a question of considerable importance, for we frame our requests in accordance with what we know of the character of the one whom we are addressing. The child with the kind, gentle and firm father does not fear to ask him for things, but deep down he enjoys the assurance that his father will not give him something which greater wisdom and experience assess as not in the child's best interests. The child with the extravagant but thoughtless father approaches him with arrogance and lays down his next demand, knowing he will not be refused. The child with the stingy, ill-tempered and abusive father will seldom ask for anything, fearing another meaningless beating.

How then shall we approach God? Jesus gives a brief but telling illustration to reinforce the main point: as sons of the kingdom we are to approach God with trust in his goodness, and persistence as we ask for the day's supply. "Which of you," Jesus asks, "if his son asks for bread, will give him a stone? Or if he asks for a fish, will give him a snake?" This scenario is desperately silly. What father would think it a fine joke to replace a bun with a stone that looked like a bun? Jesus' conclusion to his rhetorical question is inevitable: "If you, then, though you are evil, know how to give good gifts to your children, how much more will your Father in heaven give good gifts to those who ask him!" (7:9-11).

Sadly, many of God's children labor under the delusion that their heavenly Father extracts some malicious glee out of watching his children squirm now and then. Of course, they are not quite blasphemous enough to put it in such terms; but their prayer life reveals they are not thoroughly convinced of God's goodness and the love he has for them. Jesus' argument is *a fortiori*: If human fathers, who by God's standards of perfect righteousness can only be described as evil, know how to give good gifts to their children, *how much more* will God give good gifts to them who ask him? We are dealing with the God who once said to his people, "Can a mother forget the baby at her breast and have no compassion on the child she has borne? Though she may forget, I will not forget you!" (Isa. 49:15).

The Christian is to remind himself often of the sheer goodness of God, and therefore of the resources available to him from his heavenly Father:

> Come, my soul, thy suit prepare;
> Jesus loves to answer prayer;
> He himself has bid thee pray,
> Therefore will not say thee nay.
>
> Thou art coming to a King;
> Large petitions with thee bring;
> For his grace and power are such,
> None can ever ask too much.
> *John Newton (1725-1807)*

BALANCE AND PERFECTION
Matthew 7:12

I have titled this chapter, which deals with Matthew 7:1-12, "Balance and Perfection"; and those themes reach their apex in verse 12: "In everything do to others what you would have them do to you, for this sums up the Law and the Prophets."

I explained in the second chapter that 5:17-20 and 7:12 form an inclusion—that is, they bracket the main body of the Sermon on the Mount as it is recorded in Matthew, and indicate that the sermon is concerned with the way the kingdom of God fulfills the Law and the Prophets. Much of this is expounded in Matthew 5. The Old Testament, as we saw, points forward to Jesus and the kingdom he announces and finds its real continuity in them. But the righteousness demanded by the kingdom might be prostituted by some into hypocritical "acts of righteousness," and so Jesus goes on to warn against such hypocrisy in Matthew 6, insisting on sincere adherence to the perspectives of the kingdom.

At the beginning of Matthew 7, then, Jesus deals with final possible misconceptions. Precisely because he is given to preaching in absolute categories, he takes special pains to bring the parts together in balance and proportion. Of course, we do not know all Jesus said that day on the hillside in Galilee; but there is good reason to believe that Matthew has captured its thrust and balance. The first danger Jesus deals with is the danger of being judgmental (7:1-5); but he balances that against the danger of being undiscriminating (7:6). And the whole discourse is tempered by his warning against lacking a trusting persistence (7:7-11); for by this means it becomes clear that Jesus is not advocating a mere determination to improve. Rather, he is insisting that both entrance into the kingdom and progress in the kingdom require God's saving hand. Thus the whole body of the Sermon on the Mount has been rounded out and knit together with exceptional balance.

Then, Jesus caps it off with the so-called "Golden Rule." The *negative* form of this rule is known to many religions—that is, it often appears elsewhere in the form, "Do not do anything to anyone that you would not want him to do to you." For example, Rabbi Hillel taught, "What is hateful to you, do not do to your fellow creatures. That is the whole law. All else is explanation." But Jesus gives the *positive* form of this rule, and the difference between the two forms is profound. For example, the negative form would teach behavior like this: If you do not enjoy being robbed, don't rob others. If you do not like being cursed, don't curse others. If you do not enjoy being hated, don't hate others. If you do not care to be clubbed over the head, don't club others over the head. However, the positive form teaches behavior like this: If you enjoy being loved, love others. If you like to receive things, give to others. If you like being appreciated, appreciate others. The positive form is thus far more searching than its negative counterpart. Here there is no permission to withdraw into a world where I offend no one, but accomplish no positive good, either. What would you like done to you? What would you really like? Then, do that to others. Duplicate both the quality of these things, and their quantity—"in everything."

Why are we to act in this way? Jesus does *not* say that we are to do to others what we would like them to do to us *in order that* they will do it to us. At stake is no such utilitarian value as "honesty pays" or the like. Rather, the reason we are to do to others what we would like others to do to us is that such behavior sums up the Law and the Prophets. In other words, such behavior conforms to the requirements of the kingdom of God, the kingdom which is the fulfillment of the Law and the Prophets. It constitutes a quick test of the perfection demanded in 5:48; of the love described in 5:43ff.; of the truth portrayed in 5:33ff.; and so forth.

That the "Golden Rule" does not lay great stress on our relationship to

God is not really surprising. The preceding verses have already insisted on our conscious and continually formulated dependence upon him if we are to grow to meet the norms of the kingdom. Elsewhere Jesus teaches that the greatest commandment is, "Love the Lord your God with all your heart, with all your soul, and with all your mind," and that the second greatest is, "Love your neighbor as yourself" (Matt. 22:37, 39). But in Jesus' teaching it is axiomatic that the second will never be obeyed without the first: we will never love our neighbors in the way we would like to be loved until we love God with heart and soul and mind.

As the overwhelming distance between these demands and our own conduct drives home our spiritual bankruptcy, God give us a burning desire to turn to him with humble, persistent asking, seeking, knocking. Out of this we shall become "doers" of the Word, and not just "hearers."

6 MATTHEW 7:13-28

CONCLUSION:

Two Ways

Before studying Matthew 7:13-27, the conclusion of the Sermon on the Mount as it is recorded by Matthew, it may be wise to step back a pace and consider how the teaching of these chapters relates to one or two other important emphases in the New Testament. In particular, I would like to raise the question of how Matthew 5—7 meshes with major Pauline emphases, especially his stress on justification by grace through faith, preeminently expounded in his epistles to the Romans and the Galatians. I am persuaded that this pause will bring the final verses of the Sermon on the Mount into sharper focus.

❖   ❖   ❖

Excursus
The Sermon on the Mount and Pauline Emphases

Balance
Joyful Christian submission to the authority of the Scriptures brings with it commitment to a certain balance in the way we approach these Scriptures. For the Christian, the Bible is to be believed as a whole, the later revelation complementing and sometimes modifying the earlier. Within the New Testament itself, different writers stress themes which interest them or which are of particular concern to the believers among whom they minister. In giving us this sacred book, God did not choose to provide us with a textbook of systematic theology, nor a dictated letter. Rather, he sovereignly moved and inspired men to write various ac-

counts, descriptions, letters, experiences, visions, and injunctions so that what was put down was a true reflection of the human author's impressions, assessments, research, convictions, experiences—and yet at the same time the very words to God. To put it more concretely, John does not write like Paul; their vocabularies are different, their historical and theological interests differ, their styles are their own. God, however, uses both men. Because of this fact, it is not legitimate to pit one against the other, or to accept one as a normative expression of Christianity at the expense of the other.

So then, biblical revelation is not monochromatic; therefore it must not be interpreted monochromatically. Granted that this is so, we must nevertheless learn how to blend the different light rays into one unbroken spectrum.

The Sermon on the Mount contains a great deal of ethical instruction—so much so that some people have concluded that it lays out a series of conditions which must be met if a person is to enter the kingdom of God. In this view, an individual enters the kingdom because his obedience merits entrance. Such a deduction is, of course, false; we observed in the last chapter how Jesus' insistence on poverty of spirit (in 5:3), coupled with the accent on humbly petitioning God (in 7:7-11), combine to vitiate such a conclusion. However, it is understandable, to say the least, how a superficial reading of the Sermon on the Mount might lead the inattentive reader to this false conclusion.

Paul

Let us contrast Paul's teaching on salvation. In particular, let us examine three elements of that teaching. First, Paul insists that men are saved by God's free grace, and by nothing else. Certainly they cannot be saved by their works, by the merits they accumulate. He takes the first two and one half chapters of Romans to prove that all men, without exception, stand guilty before God. God is just and holy; he cannot overlook sin and pretend it doesn't matter. However, he is gracious and loving, and therefore takes no pleasure in condemning guilty people. Acting therefore in perfect conformity with both his justice and his grace, he sends his son to become a man, Jesus of Nazareth. Jesus, God's "Anointed One" (that is, God's chosen one, his "Christ"), voluntarily, as a man, obeys his Father in all things, and dies as a representative and a substitute for men who could not save themselves. God did this "to demonstrate his justice at the present time, so as to be just and the one who justifies the man who has faith in Jesus" (Rom. 3:26). "Where, then, is boasting?" Paul asks; and he replies, "It is excluded. . . . For we maintain that a man is justified by faith apart from observing the law" (Rom. 3:27f.).

Second, this salvation which comes by God's grace, through faith, does not, according to Paul, condone irresponsibility. If someone argues that God pours out his grace in proportion to the sin ("But where sin increased, grace increased all the more . . . ," Rom. 5:20) and therefore it is best to go on sinning so that grace may go on increasing, Paul will have none of it (Rom. 6:1ff.). Moreover, Paul argues further that because Jesus' death met the law's righteous demands forensically, Jesus' disciples, pardoned by their Lord's supreme act of self-sacrifice, will themselves be controlled by the Spirit of God (Rom. 8:1ff.). Indeed, *only* those who possess this Spirit, and whose lives demonstrate it, have truly been pardoned; and *all* those who possess this Spirit, and whose lives demonstrate it, have truly been pardoned.

To put it another way, the salvation which God gives by grace is not static; it inevitably results in good works. Good works may not earn salvation, but they will certainly result from it. In this connection, Ephesians 2:10 needs to be weighed alongside the more commonly-cited pair of verses preceding it: "For it is by grace you have been saved, through faith—and this not from yourselves, it is the gift of God—not by works, so that no one can boast. *For we are God's workmanship, created in Christ Jesus to do good works, which God prepared in advance for us to do*" (Eph. 2:8-10). According to this passage, good works can be construed as both the goal of salvation and the test of salvation.

Third, from the perspective of the Christian who looks back on a longer period of God's revelation than his Old Testament counterpart could, it becomes clear that the Old Testament law was never by itself designed to save anyone. It pointed forward to the salvation that was coming, and it did this in a number of ways. For example, it taught the Jews the real extent of their guilt (Rom. 2:17ff.), just as natural revelation and commonly recognized morality taught the Gentiles the extent of theirs (Rom. 1:18–2:16). As far as the Jews are concerned, the law was introduced as a stop-gap measure until the promise of redemption was fulfilled in Jesus (Gal. 3:19). Its entire sacrificial system pointed to the supreme sacrifice of the Savior himself. Thus the law, by pointing to Christ and by compounding human guilt and human awareness of that guilt, was designed to lead men to Christ, in order that they might be justified by grace, through faith (Gal. 3:24). In fact, Paul can argue that no one was ever saved by law (Gal. 3:11)—that is, by simply doing enough of what the law says.

To construct a model in which a man's good points are totted up and measured against his bad points is ridiculous from the Pauline point of view. After all, the good ought to be done without exception. Therefore there is nothing meritorious in doing good and obeying God's law; and failure to do good (that is, breaking God's law) is such unequivocal evil that we have no means of making it up. That by which we would like to think we can make it up—viz., doing good—we are supposed to do anyway; and so it can scarcely atone for the evil. Paul argues that even before Christ came, and the real object of faith was fully unveiled to our view, Old Testament believers were acceptable to God only on the basis of his grace. The law looked forward to Christ's cross and resurrection, somewhat the way the gospel now looks back on those climactic events. Old Testament believers, even while seeking to obey the formal law, had to approach God by faith—in poverty of spirit, desiring divine grace—or not at all.

Current Christianity

Of course, Paul is referring primarily to the function of law within the history of the Jewish race. However, this account of things also holds up at the personal level. It is usually true that a man won't cry to be found until he knows or suspects he's lost. He won't beg for pardon until he thinks he's condemned. He will not ask for forgiveness until he is conscious of his guilt. I am aware, of course, that some people become Christians without passing through deep traumas in these areas; but I suspect some of the same features apply anyway. For example, some are converted because they are drawn by the humbling magnificence of Jesus' love, as expressed in his self-sacrifice. But that means they recognize some need in their own lives, or some claim he has on them, or an essential superiority in him which they admit they do not possess and would like to establish as their goal. And these people, I suspect, do not make up the majority of genuine conversions. To go farther, I would argue that the reason we are currently seeing such an embarrassingly high percentage of spurious conversions to Christ is precisely because we have not first taught people their need of Christ.

In one of his letters to a young man who wanted to know how to preach the gospel, John Wesley offers a quite different approach. He says that whenever he arrived at any new place to preach the gospel, he began with a general declaration of the love of God. Then he preached "the law" (by which he meant all of God's righteous standards and the penalty of disobedience) as searchingly as he could. This he kept up until a large proportion of his hearers found themselves under deep conviction of sin, beginning even to despair of the possibility of forgiveness from this holy God. Then, and only then, did he introduce the good news of Jesus Christ. Wesley explained the saving significance of Christ's person, ministry, death, and resurrection, and the wonderful truth that salvation is solely by God's grace, through faith. Unless his audiences sensed that they were guilty, and quite helpless to save themselves, the wonder and availability of God's grace would leave them unmoved. Wesley adds that after quite a number had been converted, he would mix in more themes connected with "law." He did this to underline the truth that genuine believers hunger for experiential righteousness, and continue to acknowledge poverty of spirit, recognizing constantly that their acceptance with God depends always and only on Christ's sacrifice.

In much contemporary evangelism, there is little concern for whether or not God will accept us, and much concern for whether or not we will accept him. Little attention is paid to whether or not we please him, and much to whether or not he pleases us. Many popular evangelistic methods are molded by these considerations. As a result, there is far too little stress on God's character and the requirements of the kingdom, and far too much stress on our needs. Worse, our needs are cast in preeminently psychological categories, not moral ones (alienation and loneliness, not bitterness and self-seeking and hatred; frustration and fear, not prayerlessness and unbelief). To top it off, peace, joy, and love are preached as desirable goals. These *are* desirable, but they suffer from two defects. First, virtues such as peace, joy, and love can easily be interpreted in merely personal, almost mystical terms. As a result, the biblical emphases on peace *with God* and with men, joy *in the Lord*, and tough-minded love which gives sacrificially to both God and men, are reduced to a warm, pleasant glow. Second, these virtues need to be set alongside complementary virtues such as justice, integrity, righteousness, truth, humility, and faith.

Imagine a large cone:

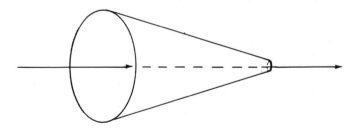

If the entrance to the kingdom is presented as large and wide, many people will take the first steps. However, they soon discover that the cone narrows down inside. To continue would mean lightening the load they are carrying; the final terms for entrance are very restrictive. They have been induced to enter the cone by much talk of life, forgiveness, peace, and joy; and suddenly they discover more confining notions. They learn of sin and repentance, obedience and discipleship. Not surprisingly, there is often an eruption and they blow back out.

But the cone might face the other way:

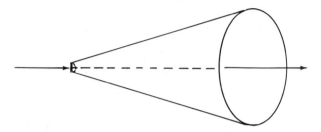

Now, the entrance seems very narrow. There is no admittance until a person comes without any baggage. He enters solely on the conditions laid down. But once inside, to his delight he discovers expanding horizons and growing freedom.

Paul, we have seen, understands that in general the cone lies in the second position. He explains that one of the major functions of the law is to condemn men. That is, far from providing a convenient code by which men may earn merits before God, the law functions to expose sin and condemn it. Paul writes, "Now we know that whatever the law says, it says to those who are under the law, so that every mouth may be silenced and the whole world held accountable to God. Therefore no one will be declared righteous in his sight by observing the law; rather, through the law we become conscious of sin" (Rom. 3:19f.). As a result, when a person comes to Christ, he comes stripped of all pretense of self-righteousness, all claims to personal moral merit. I am not saying that a person is worthless. Far from it—each person is made in the image of God and therefore possesses immense significance, not the least of which is his eternal destiny. But before God no one possesses any *meritorious moral worth* that would earn him forgiveness, salvation, and entrance to the kingdom of God.

In other words, it is typical of Paul to stress, on the one hand, salvation by grace through faith; and, on the other, the unequivocal surrender by which men must approach God.

Christ

How often does Jesus' own ministry reflect the same perspectives! He has an uncanny knack of putting his finger on the sorest spot or the biggest hindrance in the life of the person with whom he is dealing. The rich ruler, in love with his wealth, needs to get rid of it (Luke 18:18ff.). The Samaritan woman is prepared to talk about religion, but Jesus brings up her adulterous relationships (John 4:7ff.). He warns prospective disciples to count the cost (Luke 14:25ff.), concluding his illustrations of this point with the penetrating statement, "In the same way, any of you who does not give up everything he has cannot be my disciple" (Luke 14:33). There it is—the narrow end of the cone. This idea emerges again when he actually rebuffs half-hearted or premature volunteers (Luke 9:57-62).

Of course, this is only one side of the picture. Jesus can also be found giving broad invitations (see Matt. 11:28-30; John 7:37f.); and he is known as the one who will not break bruised reeds nor quench smoldering wicks (Matt. 12:20). But this only means that to the crushed, bruised, downtrodden, and weary he shows himself to be gracious. Jesus is called as a doctor to the sick, not the well; as a Savior for sinners, not for the righteous (Matt. 9:12f.). The broken people do not need large lessons on poverty of spirit: they've already learned them, and now need words of grace and hope.

I am coming now to the nub of the issue, as far as the Sermon on the Mount is concerned. Paul makes it clear that the law makes men conscious of sin, that men are saved by grace through faith, and that no one is acceptable to God if he brings along conditions and caveats. Paul *explains* the function of law; and *what Paul is explaining in Romans and Galatians, Jesus is doing in the Sermon on the Mount.*

It is not for nothing that the Sermon on the Mount begins with the demand for poverty of spirit. It begins by demanding that kingdom hopefuls acknowledge their spiritual bankruptcy, their need. Moreover, just as Paul is explaining some of the relationships between law and the gospel, so also is Jesus (cf. Matt. 5:17-20); but he does so in such a way as to underscore the demand for righteousness in the kingdom. Whatever binding authority Old Testament law still possesses, it possesses in that which has fulfilled it, that is, in the kindgom. Therefore in one sense Jesus is preaching the law: he is preaching that toward which the law and the prophets pointed. In thus proclaiming the norms and requirements of the kingdom, he is simultaneously providing genuine disciples with the kingdom's perspectives, and making all others painfully aware of their insurmountable shortcomings.

Of course, Jesus is preaching to people who still have not wrestled with the significance of his death, nor rejoiced at the historical fact and eschatological dimensions of his resurrection. This pre-Passion setting undoubtedly influences how much Jesus tells them, and in what terms. Nevertheless, I insist that if the Sermon on the Mount be construed merely as legal requirement to kingdom entrance, no one shall ever enter: can anyone meditate long on Matthew 5–7 and remain unashamed? The Sermon on the Mount provides us with a crushing blow to self-righteousness, and follows it up with an invitation to petition God for favor (7:7-11), without which there can be no admittance to the kingdom. At the same time it sketches in the quality of life of those who do enter, those who petition God (7:7-11), ask for forgiveness (6:12), and who by God's grace discover not only forgiveness but a growing personal conformity to kingdom norms. It is not long before their own lives begin to sum up the law and the prophets.

❀   ❀   ❀

Nothing could be more calamitous than to meditate long and hard on Matthew 5:1—7:12 and then to resolve to improve a little. The discipleship which Jesus requires is absolute, radical in the (etymological) sense that it gets to the root of human conduct and to the root of relationships between God and men. A person either enters the kingdom or he does not. He walks the road that leads to life, or he walks the road that leads to destruction. There is no third alternative. Nothing, nothing at all, could have more crucial significance than following Jesus. Even if today this is far from being a universally admitted truth, yet one day all men without exception shall confess it, some to their everlasting grief.

Jesus therefore concludes the Sermon on the Mount with a number of paired alternatives. He speaks of two paths (7:13f.), two trees (7:15-20), two claims (7:21-23), two houses (7:24-27). By these pairs he insists that there are two ways, and only two. These final verses of the Sermon on the Mount demand decision and commitment of the type that beseeches God for mercy and pardon. Such discipleship is characterized by that deep repentance which hungers for nothing more than conformity to God's will. But because there are only two ways, simple failure to make such deep commitment is already a commitment not to do so. Jesus' way demands repentance, trust, and obedience. Therefore refusal, stemming as it must from an unrepentant arrogance, unbelief and/or disobedience—in short, self-centeredness instead of God-centeredness—can only be construed as rebellion.

Two ways, and only two. The Sermon on the Mount does not end with lofty thoughts of human goodness, sprinkled liberally with naive hope about the inevitability of human progress. It offers two ways, and only two. The one ends in life (7:14), good fruit (7:17), entrance into the kingdom of heaven (7:21), stability (7:25); the other ends in destruction (7:13), bad fruit and fire (7:19), exclusion from the kingdom along with other evildoers (7:23), ruination (7:27). Solemn thoughts, these; a man will ignore the weight of these blessings and curses only at his own eternal peril.

TWO PATHS
Matthew 7:13f

Jesus says, first of all, "Enter through the narrow gate. For wide is the gate and broad is the road that leads to destruction, and many enter through it. But small is the gate and narrow the road that leads to life, and only a few find it" (7:13f.).

The metaphor is straightforward enough. We are to picture two paths, two roadways. The first is broad (not "easy," RSV) and its gate is wide. It accommodates many people, all enjoying its spacious contours. But although it is so well-traveled, it ends in destruction. The other path is narrow, and the way into it is small. It is confined, and relatively few travelers are to be found on it. But it leads to "life"—a synonym for the kingdom.

What legitimate deductions can be drawn from these two verses? I shall mention five things. First, God's way is not spacious, but confining. Poverty of spirit is not easy; prayer is not easy; righteousness is not easy; transformed God-centered attitudes are not easily achieved. In fact, these things are impossible for us, apart from God's grace. They are alien to much of what is in us and which cries out to be heard; and therefore the re-alignment that is part and parcel of genuine conversion is a confining thing. There is no room for me to set my opinion against the Lord's, no room to set goals in any way at cross purposes to his, no room to form attachments which vie for the central place the Lord Jesus must have.

There is considerable danger that the picture I am painting will be thought dull gray, not to say morbid; and so I hasten to add certain caveats to what I have just said. There is a whole spectrum of joys and freedoms for the Christian. The deepest joy is joy in personally knowing God through Christ, just as the deepest human joys have always been close, personal friendships. There is the liberty of sins forgiven and of progressive triumph over temptation. New loves and friendships mushroom with other disciples of Christ, so much so that Jesus can say, "I tell you the truth, no one who has left home or brothers or sisters or mother or father or children or fields for me and the gospel will fail to receive a hundred times as much in this present age (homes, brothers, sisters, mothers, children and fields—and with them, persecutions) and in the age to come, eternal life" (Mark 10:29f.). As the Godhead becomes the center of the Christian's thinking, all of life takes on a new and fascinating attraction as he glimpses the wholeness of things under God.

> Heaven above is softer blue,
> Earth around is sweeter green;
> Something lives in every hue

Christless eyes have never seen:
Birds with gladder songs o'erflow,
Flowers with deeper beauties shine,
Since I know, as now I know,
I am His, and He is mine.
George W. Robinson (1838–1877)

Yet the way is confining nevertheless. Indeed, the more hesitation there is about going Christ's way wholeheartedly, without reserve, the more confining his way seems. However, the more enthusiasm there is for following him regardless of personal opinion or peer pressure, regardless of cost, the more liberating his way appears.

Second, we may deduce from Matthew 7:13f. that God's way cannot be discovered by appeal to majority opinion, for the majority is on the road that leads to destruction. Christians will apply Paul's words to many perspectives: "Let God be true, and every man a liar" (Rom. 3:4). If someone asks directly, "Does this mean that only relatively few will be saved, and that the rest are lost?" then the safest answer is that of Jesus himself (Luke 13:22-30):

[22]Then Jesus went through the cities and villages, teaching as he made his way to Jerusalem. [23]Someone asked him, "Lord, are only a few people going to be saved?"

He said to them, [24]"Make every effort to enter through the narrow door, because many, I tell you, will try to enter and will not be able to. [25]Once the owner of the house gets up and closes the door, you will stand outside knocking and pleading, 'Sir, open the door for us.'

"But he will answer, 'I don't know you or where you come from.'

[26]"Then you will say, 'We ate and drank with you, and you taught in our streets.'

[27]"But he will reply, 'I don't know you or where you come from. Away from me, all you evildoers!'

[28]"There will be weeping and grinding of teeth when you see Abraham, Isaac and Jacob and all the prophets in the kingdom of God, but you yourselves thrown out. [29]People will come from east and west and north and south, and will take their places at the feast in the kingdom of God. [30]Indeed there are those who are last who will be first, and first who will be last."

Strong words! They were spoken first of all to the Jews of Jesus' own day who were rejecting their own Messiah; but the thrust of Jesus' response will not change. He demands of his questioners less speculation on the precise number of those who are "going to be saved," and more personal concern about their own salvation.

In the third place, it follows that the narrow way to life cannot be pursued as long as we are motivated by a desire to please the mass of men. Most men travel the broad road; the narrow road is a little lonelier.

This is another way of expressing a truth which emerges repeatedly in the Sermon on the Mount, that true disciples of Jesus will not play to the galleries, nor form their values according to the passing approval of faddish whim. The beatitudes tell us that it is God's approval alone which is of ultimate importance. In Matthew 6 Jesus excoriates that form of hypocrisy which practices piety to win the approval of men. And here in Matthew 7 he tells us that the way to life is narrow and not as popular as the way to destruction.

"Choose for yourselves today whom you will serve . . . ; but as for me and my household, we will serve the Lord" (Josh. 24:15). Joshua's challenge to Israel comes to us today with the same vigor, a vigor born of clear-headed analysis. It reminds me of the spirit of Athanasius, the fourth-century theologian who for awhile stood virtually alone in his defense of the deity of Christ. His work has largely stood the test of time; and in his own time he eventually won the day. But during the darker periods when he was being sucked into the maelstrom of theological controversy and seemed to be isolated from his friends and colleagues, he was advised to give up his opinions because the whole world was against him. His reply was devastatingly simple: "Then is Athanasius against the whole world."

Of course, it is possible to take such a position out of sheer arrogance and stubborn independence. Anyone who stoops to such obnoxious egotism has not learned even the first lessons of the Sermon on the Mount. The distinctions by which such a person seeks to preserve his isolation are more traditional and personal than biblical. Nevertheless, when all allowances have been made, it remains a fact that the narrow way wins few popularity contests. This is so partly because the full-blooded righteousness of the Sermon on the Mount is too comprehensive and demanding to be universally attractive to a race that prefers compromise and assorted personal corruptions. Also, the Sermon's concern for truth is so great that personal intolerance of false teaching is necessarily entailed (as we shall see in Matt. 7:15-20).

In the fourth place, the two paths are not ends in themselves, but have eternal significance beyond themselves. The one ends in destruction, the other in life. Ironically, it is the spacious and popular path which leads to destruction, and the confined and relatively unpopular one which leads to life. The point remains the same in each case; not the path but the path's destination is of ultimate significance. The tragedy is that otherwise reasonable men become so enamored with the spaciousness and the popularity of their path that they take little thought as to its destination. Should they hear that it leads to destruction, they will deny it, arguing that they are no worse than most others on the same road, and that in any case God would not permit the destruction of so many. Let me state emphatically that the Scriptures do not encourage such optimism. Jesus himself insists that only the narrow way leads to life. Only the path that seems confining explodes in the end into vitality, the consummation of the kingdom of God.

Lastly, let it be noted once more that there are only two ways. To put this point in other terms, we might say that there is no other way to life, no other way to avoid destruction, than the narrow way. Men will not gain the kingdom by worshiping nature, nor by pious sentiment, nor by drifting into salvation without decision and commitment, still less by hedonism and self-expression. They will enter life by coming under the kingdom's norms, and be saved by God's grace through faith in Christ, or they will head for destruction. On this point Jesus insists.

TWO TREES
Matthew 7:15-20

Disciples of Jesus Christ are not very susceptible to open invitations to sin. They are not likely to be taken in by the teacher/preacher who advocates raw hedonism, anarchy, or various forms of unbelief. The problem will lie with the preacher who seems pious, who prays, who at first glance seems to have all the marks of the Christian. He uses all the right religious clichés, and the very dogmatism he exudes seems to testify to his orthodoxy. He appears as one of the sheep in Christ's flock, and most of the genuine sheep fail to notice he is really a savage wolf. "Watch out for false prophets," Jesus warns. "They come to you in sheep's clothing, but inwardly they are ferocious wolves" (7:15).

The problem of false prophets has always been with us. A prophet is fundamentally a messenger for someone else, and these false prophets claim to be speaking for God. The acuteness of the danger they present is that they are accepted at face value—they appear within the church and gather a following within the church. Elsewhere Jesus warns that "many false prophets will appear and deceive many people" (Matt. 24:11). Toward the end of his ministry, the apostle Paul warned the elders of the church in Ephesus, "I know that after I leave, savage wolves will come in among you and will not spare the flock. *Even from your own number* men will arise and distort the truth in order to draw away disciples after them. So be on your guard! Remember that for three years I never stopped warning each of you night and day with tears" (Acts 20:29-31). Or consider the solemn words in II Peter 2:1-3, 17-22:

> [1]But there were also false prophets among the people, just as there will be false teachers among you. They will secretly introduce destructive here-

sies, even denying the sovereign Lord who bought them—bringing swift destruction on themselves. ²Many will follow their shameful ways and will bring the way of truth into disrepute. ³In their greed these teachers will exploit you with stories they have made up. Their condemnation has long been hanging over them, and their destruction has not been sleeping.

¹⁷These men are springs without water and mists driven by a storm. Blackest darkness is reserved for them. ¹⁸For they mouth empty, boastful words and, by appealing to the lustful desires of sinful human nature, they entice people who are just escaping from those who live in error. ¹⁹They promise them freedom, while they themselves are slaves of depravity—for a man is a slave to whatever has mastered him. ²⁰If they have escaped the corruption of the world by knowing our Lord and Savior Jesus Christ and are again entangled in it and overcome, they are worse off at the end than they were at the beginning. ²¹It would have been better for them not to have known the way of righteousness, than to have known it and then to turn their backs on the sacred commandment that was passed on to them. ²²Of them the proverbs are true: "A dog returns to its vomit," and, "A sow that is washed goes back to her wallowing in the mud."

Perhaps we should not be surprised, if we remember the archetype behind these false prophets. Paul, writing of certain men with whom he had to deal, unveils their real model: "For such men are false prophets, deceitful workmen, masquerading as apostles of Christ. And no wonder, for Satan himself masquerades as an angel of light. It is not surprising, then, if his servants masquerade as servants of righteousness. Their end will be what their actions deserve" (II Cor. 11:13-15).

How, then, are we to recognize these wolves in sheep's clothing? Many suggestions for unmasking them are scattered throughout the Scriptures, but only two are in view here.

The first is based on a contextual observation. Within the context of the Sermon on the Mount, the false prophet can only be someone who does not advocate the narrow way presented by Jesus. He may not be wildly heretical in other areas; indeed, he may set himself up as a staunch defender of orthodoxy. But the way which he commends is not narrow or disturbing, and therefore he can gain quite a hearing. These people remind me of certain religio-political prophets in the time of Jeremiah, concerning whom God says, "For from the least of them even to the greatest of them, every one is covetous, and from the prophet even to the priest, every one deals falsely. And they have healed the wound of my people slightly, saying 'Peace, peace,'—but there is no peace. Were they ashamed because of the abomination they have done? They were not even ashamed at all; they did not even know how to blush" (Jer. 6:13-15; cf. Jer. 8:8-12). There is nothing in their preaching which fosters poverty of spirit, nothing which searches the conscience and makes men cry to God for mercy, nothing which excoriates all forms of religious hypocrisy, nothing which prompts such righteousness of conduct and attitude that some persecution is inevitable. It is even possible in some instances that everything these false prophets say is true; but because they leave out the difficult bits, they do not tell the whole truth, and their total message is false.

The second test is not based on contextual observations, but on the explicit argument of the text. Jesus says, "By their fruit you will recognize them. Do people pick grapes from thornbushes, or figs from thistles? Likewise every good tree bears good fruit, but a bad tree bears bad fruit. A good tree cannot bear bad fruit, and a bad tree cannot bear good fruit. Every tree that does not bear good fruit is cut down and thrown into the fire. Thus, by their fruit you will recognize them" (7:16-20).

This semitic way of putting things (that is, both positively and negatively: every good tree bears good fruit, no good tree bears bad fruit, and so forth) makes the test very sure. In Jesus' day, everyone knew that the buckthorn had little black berries which could be mistaken for grapes, and that there was a thistle whose flower, from a distance, might be mistaken for a fig. But no one would confuse the buckthorn and the grape once he started to use the fruit to make some wine. No one would be taken in by thistle flowers when it came to eating figs for supper.

In other words, from a certain perspective, false prophets can look like real prophets, and even their fruit may appear to be genuine. But the nature of the false prophet cannot be hidden forever: sooner or later he will be seen for what he is. Just as he does not advocate Jesus' narrow way, so also does he fail to live it; this fact must one day be exposed to all who cherish the narrow way. In this manner, Matthew 7:15-20 serves as a bridge between 7:13f. and 7:21-23. Matthew 7:13f. deals with the two ways; 7:21-23 (as we shall see) pictures a man who has all the trappings of discipleship to Jesus but is not characterized by obedience to Jesus. The bridge (7:15-20) presents false prophets who do not teach the narrow way, nor practice it. The falseness of their teaching erupts in the disobedience of their lives.

I must emphasize that Jesus is not encouraging a heresy-hunting mentality here. After all, the same Jesus has only recently condemned judgmental attitudes. Yet false teachers must be identified. If they are not recognized immediately by their doctrine, then sooner or later they may be recognized by their lives; for what a man believes must sooner or later manifest itself in what he does. Jesus affirms an indissoluble link between belief and conduct. Moreover, these verses are not as much given to threaten the false prophets themselves (even though the bad trees are cast into the fire), as to encourage ordinary disciples to spot them: "By their fruit you will recognize them."

This test must not be superficially applied. It will not do to use only this text, find some socially useful pagan and regard him as a true prophet. Still less will it suffice to adopt secular criteria by which to assess a man's fruit: success, style, aplomb, popularity. Nor will patterns of speech and conduct acceptable to contemporary evangelicalism suffice. The fruit the Lord Jesus looks for is a life in growing conformity to the norms of the kingdom: righteousness, transparent humility, purity, trusting and persistent prayerfulness, obedience to Jesus' words, truthfulness, love, generosity, rejection of all that is hypocritical. It may take time for the test to prove very helpful; but where doctrinal aberration cannot be detected immediately and unequivocally, the "fruit test" is eventually a safe guide.

This is a day when pluralism is popular. However, although everyone may have the right to his own opinion, it does not follow that every opinion is right. To some it will appear terribly intolerant even to speak of "false" prophets; yet that is Jesus' designation of would-be spokesmen for God who do not teach what Jesus himself teaches. "Watch out for false prophets," he says; "by their fruit you will recognize them." The kingdom of God is the issue. Failure to heed Jesus' warning means that the threat of judgment looming over the heads of the false teachers becomes a threat to others as well. Not only their destiny, but ours, yours and mine, are at risk, if we fail to identify and avoid the false prophets.

TWO CLAIMS
Matthew 7:21-23

"Not everyone who says to me, 'Lord, Lord,' will enter the kingdom of heaven, but only the one who does the will of my Father who is in heaven. Many will say to me on that day, 'Lord, Lord, did we not prophesy in your name, and in your name drive out demons and perform many miracles?' Then I will tell them plainly, 'I never knew you. Away from me, you evildoers!" (7:21-23).

Two claims are made, and two kinds of claimants are portrayed. The first group approaches Jesus reverently on "that day, the day of judgment; and they address him as "Lord." Probably their belief is perfectly orthodox. Moreover, they have an impressive record of spiritual experience. They have prophesied in Jesus' name, they have exorcised demons in Jesus' name, and in Jesus' name performed many miracles. The Lord does not deny any of their claims, and neither should we. We may therefore expect that even in our own day there are *many* (7:22) people who use the right language and who have performed spiritual wonders in Jesus' name, but who are not genuine disciples. One of the most tragic ingredients to this scenario is the way these people take themselves to be genuine believers. They clearly expect admission to the consummated kingdom.

Sometimes, of course, people who attempt using Jesus' name to do various things get caught long before the last judgment. In Acts 19, for example, the seven silly sons of Sceva are exposed for the charlatans they are. For their pains they get beaten up and chased down the street by one particularly aggressive demon. Whether now or on the day of judgment, the false claimants will be exposed. Eventually Jesus will disown them: "I never knew you." He will banish them from his presence: "Away from me." And he will dismiss them as "evildoers," literally as those who practice lawlessness.

What, then, is the *essential* characteristic of the true believer, the genuine disciple of Jesus Christ? It is not loud profession, nor spectacular spiritual triumphs, nor protestations of great spiritual experience. Rather, his chief characteristic is obedience. True believers perform the will of their Father, consistent with their prayer, "Your will be done on earth as in heaven." They cannot forget that at the beginning of the Sermon on the Mount, Jesus said, "Anyone who breaks one of the least of these commandments and teaches others to do the same will be called least in the kingdom of heaven, but whoever practices and teaches these commands will be called great in the kingdom of heaven. For I tell you that unless your righteousness surpasses that of the Pharisees and the teachers of the law, you will certainly not enter the kingdom of heaven" (5:19f.). And so they practice obedience. The Father's will is not simply admired, discussed, praised, debated; it is done. It is not theologically analyzed, nor congratulated for its high ethical tones; it is done. The test is rephrased by a famous second-century document, the *Didache*, which says, "But not everyone who speaks in the Spirit is a prophet, except he have the behavior of the Lord."

There are several different ways to become self-deluded about spiritual things. For example, it is possible to enjoy some sort of unique spiritual experience and live in its glow at the expense of *ongoing* spiritual experience and sustained practical obedience. I heard of a man who enjoyed what he took to be a special outpouring of God's blessing upon him. He felt himself transported with Paul to the third heaven. So momentous was the event that he wrote it all up in a paper to which he gave the title, "My Experience." The months slipped past, and he became indifferent to spiritual things. At first he preserved the form, and hauled out his manuscript to show various visitors. But as months turned into years, even the form of godliness was abandoned, and his experience lay forgotten in a dusty drawer. Many years later a minister came calling. The man, thinking to impress his visitor, called upstairs to his wife, asking her to bring down "My Experience." She rummaged around until she found the tattered document, and replied, "I'm sorry, dear, but your experience is rather moth-eaten." Just so: the man had lulled himself into irresponsible spiritual apathy by coasting along on the memory of some past experience.

Another form of self-delusion, however, is evident in Matthrew 7:21-23. It is not so much that the false claimant lulls himself into spiritual apathy, as that he mistakes loud profession and supernatural, almost magical formulations and experiences, for true spirituality and genuine godliness. Obedience is neglected. The pressure of the spectacular has excluded the stability of growing conformity to the Father's will. Because he seems to be getting results, immediate results, spectacular results, he feels he is close to the center of true religion. His success indices are soaring: God must be blessing him. Surely God will understand and sympathize if there is not always enough time for prayer, self-examination, or conscious repentance. The results are the important thing. If the truth gets a trifle bent, it's only because the supporters need to hear certain things. And is it wise to run the risk of driving off such supporters by talking about the narrow way? Just as Nixon's closest aides could talk themselves into believing that their cause was more important than their ethics, so these religious extroverts convince themselves that their success-oriented spectacular victories are more important than the nitty-gritty of consistent discipleship.

It is true, of course, that no man enters the kingdom because of his obedience; but it is equally true that no man enters the kingdom who is not obedient. It is true that men are saved by God's grace through faith in Christ; but it is equally true that God's grace in a man's life inevitably results in obedience. Any other view of grace cheapens grace, and turns it into something unrecognizable. Cheap grace preaches forgiveness without repentance, church membership without rigorous church discipline, discipleship without obedience, blessing without persecution, joy without righteousness, results without obedience. In the entire history of the church, has there ever been another generation with so many nominal Christians and so few real (i.e., obedient) ones? And where nominal Christianity is compounded by spectacular profession, it is especially likely to manufacture its own false assurance.

TWO HOUSES
Matthew 7:24-27

Entrance into the kingdom, then, does turn on obedience after all—not the obedience which earns merit points, but which bows to Jesus' lordship in everything and without reservation. Such obedience necessarily blends with genuine repentance, making the two almost one. Within this framework, the issue of obedience is everything. The previous verses have just shown this to be so; and now Jesus draws the Sermon on the Mount to a close with a paragraph introduced by a telling "Therefore." Because only the one who *does* the will of his Father will enter the kingdom, Jesus says—

> [24]"*Therefore*, everyone who hears these words of mine and puts them into practice is like a wise man who built his house on the rock. [25]The rain came down, the streams rose, and the winds blew and beat against that house; yet it did not fall, because it had its foundation on the rock. [26]But everyone who hears these words of mine and does not put them into practice is like a foolish man who built his house on sand. [27]The rain came down, the streams rose, and the winds blew and beat against that house, and it fell with a great crash" (Matt. 7:24-27).

Picture these two houses. There may not be much in their external appearance to enable the casual observer to distinguish between them. Both seem attractive and clean, freshly-painted perhaps. One, however, has its foundation resting securely on bedrock; the other has as its foundation nothing more substantial than sand. Only the most severe storm will betray the difference; but granted the storm, the betrayal is inevitable.

The image of the "foundation" is variously used in Scripture. For example, God's personal knowledge of his own people is said to be a divine foundation, providing his people with confidence (II Tim. 2:19). Good works are a foundation for the coming age, not so much in the sense that they earn life as in the sense that without them there is no life (I Tim. 6:17-19). But most commonly, Jesus himself is the foundation, a sure foundation. Prophesied in the Old Testament (Isa. 28:16), he comes in the New to be the certain basis of assurance for his people. In this sense, as Peter wisely discerns, there is salvation in none other (Acts 4:12): Jesus Christ himself, in his person and his mission, is the sole foundation.

Nevertheless, Jesus is not the foundation referred to in Matthew 7:24-27. In fact, the focus is not quite centered on the foundations adopted, rock and sand, but upon the two builders and their entire projects. The man who builds his house upon a shifting foundation is likened to the person who hears Jesus' words but who does not put them into practice. The man who builds his house upon a rock is likened to the person who not only hears Jesus' words but also puts them into practice. The difference between the two houses is therefore to be likened to the difference between obedience and disobedience.

The rock in this extended metaphor may well represent Jesus' words: "These words of mine," Jesus twice says, the "of mine" quite emphatic. The expression harks back to the repeated and authoritative refrain,

"You have heard . . . but I tell you." Perhaps there is a further nuance. These words are especially Jesus' words in the sense that his own life is perfectly congruent with his words. I who pen these lines may repeat Jesus' words, but I remain a sinner like you who read them. In that sense, Jesus' words are not my words; they are only his. Putting those words into practice, then, is like building a house on a sure foundation. The other man builds a superstructure, and no more.

The violent storm differentiates between the two buildings. In the Old Testament, and also elsewhere in Jewish writings, the storm sometimes serves as a symbol for God's judgment (see Ezek. 13:10ff.), especially God's eschatological judgment, his final judgment. No power was more certain to evoke fear in pre-nuclear man than the unleashed fury of nature's violence—the symbol was therefore apt.

This is the place to pause and reflect on the threats Jesus has been issuing. In 7:13f. He promises destruction for those who travel the broad way. This is followed first by a picture of a fire burning up unproductive branches (7:15-20), and then by a categorical rejection of the disobedient (7:21-23). These are now capped by likening a man who hears Jesus' words and who does not practice them, to a house shattered, pulverized and swept away by a vicious storm. The question will not be restrained: Is Jesus trying to frighten people into the kingdom?

In one sense, of course, the answer must be yes. Some people may well be drawn to Christ because of the attraction of forgiveness; others may feel the first stirrings of desire to follow him when they first glimpse the immensity of his love or the integrity of his life, or when they experience the shame engendered by his scrutiny. But not a few will come only because they see that the issues with which Jesus is concerned are eternal issues—ultimately, nothing less then heaven and hell. Indeed, Jesus' teaching has important things to say about race relations, social justice, and personal integrity; but it cannot be fairly reduced to the temporal concerns of my lifetime here. There is a heaven to be gained and a hell to be shunned.

If you are sleeping soundly in a house desperately threatened by rising flood waters, you may thank me for pounding at your door to rouse you. At the very least, you are not likely to accuse me of frightening you into safety. Frighten you I shall, effect your removal to a safe place I may attempt: but you would not *accuse* me of "frightening you into safety." If you were so attached to your home you could not bear to leave it, you might conceivably choose to stay with it and run the risk of perishing; or if you remained honestly oblivious to the danger you might dismiss me as a fool. But while I tried to frighten you to safety, you would not *accuse* me of doing so.

Similarly, Jesus concludes the Sermon on the Mount by honestly attempting to frighten men and women into the kingdom, into salvation. You may not believe that a hell exists. In that case, you may dismiss Jesus as a liar or a fool. Alternatively, you may be so attached to your sin that even the threat of final and catastrophic judgment may not induce you to leave it. But you will be foolish indeed if you simply accuse Jesus of frightening you into the kingdom.

The real issue is the truth behind Jesus' words, the truth which prompts Jesus' warning. Either there is a hell to be shunned, or there is not. If there is not, then Jesus' entire credibility is shattered, for he himself speaks twice as often of hell as of heaven. The pages of the Bible strain metaphor and exhaust the resources of language in describing the holy delights of the new heaven and the new earth, still to come; but they scarcely do less in outlining the horrors and terrors of hell. It is variously described as the place of outer darkness, the place where the worm will not die, the place of exclusion and rejection, the place of burning and torment, the place where there will be weeping and grinding of teeth. I am not trying to give you hell's coordinates, nor place it on a map. Just as I find myself unable to describe the new heaven and earth except in the metaphors of Scripture, so I cannot describe hell except in the metaphors of Scripture. But those metaphors are staggering.

Whether you accept the existence of hell will depend in large part upon your total estimate of the person and ministry of Jesus. If you can dismiss him, you will have little difficulty dismissing hell. If you claim to follow him, then you cannot with integrity do so in a subjective way which avoids the inconvenient and unpleasant.*

My chief concern, however, is not to wax polemical on the subject of judgment and hell, but to assist others in coming to a straightforward understanding of the Sermon on the Mount. The Sermon ends with the threat of judgment. The four sections which make up the conclusion of these three chapters concur in this theme. In fact, these four paragraphs, despite the diversity of their metaphors, each stresses two unyielding themes. The first is that there are only two ways, one which ends in the kingdom of God and the other in destruction. The second theme is that the former way is characterized by obedience to Jesus and practical conformity to *all* his teaching.

These pronouncements ought to instill in us a holy fear. Which one of us stands unashamed beside the precepts of the Sermon on the Mount?

---

*If you need more information about Jesus Christ, or about the New Testament documents which constitute our primary sources concerning him, I recommend two books in particular: *Basic Christianity*, by John R. W. Scott; and *The New Testament Documents: Are They Reliable?*, by F. F. Bruce.

Do not these threats of judgment prompt poverty of spirit, which is the first of the kingdom's norms?

We do well to remember that Paul is writing truth when he insists that men are saved only because Christ acted as their substitute and died in their behalf. Christianity is not simply a moralistic religion of high ideals. High ideals—indeed, the highest—it has; but it also presents a crucified yet risen Savior who forgives repentant men and then gives them life to grow to meet those ideals.

We ought not forget that Matthew's record of the Sermon on the Mount must be taken in the context of his entire Gospel. It is not for nothing that his Gospel begins with a prophecy concerning Jesus which stresses his function *as a Savior*: "She [Mary] will give birth to a son, and you [Joseph] are to give him the name Jesus, because he will save his people from their sins" (Matt. 1:21). Within this context, the Sermon on the Mount does not press men and women to despair, still less to self-salvation. Rather, it presses men and women to Jesus. The Sermon on the Mount reflects no malicious glee at the prospect of perdition, no cheer at consigning so many to destruction. The warning is, in fact, entreaty.

May God grant his people a spirit of contrition which petitions him for grace and forgiveness by Jesus Christ, and a growing conformity to the norms and perspectives of the kingdom.

✿   ✿   ✿

The Sermon ends. "When Jesus had finished saying these things, the crowds were amazed at his teaching, because he taught as one who had authority, and not as their teachers of the law" (Matt. 7:28f.).

The teachers of the law taught derivatively, that is, by referring to the authorities. But Jesus taught with his own authority. All of us are impressed by the man whose skill and knowledge of a subject are so outstanding that he clears away the rubble of misconception and outlines the truth of the matter with sharp, incisive strokes. This was the effect Jesus had on his first hearers.

Those hearers were amazed at Jesus. Perhaps that is part of coming to him, part of the necessary recognition of his authority. May God in his mercy grant that we will not stop at mere amazement, but press on to that deeply rooted commitment which sings:

> Be Thou my Vision, O Lord of my heart;
> Naught be all else to me, save that Thou art—
> Thou my best thought, by day or by night,
> Waking or sleeping, Thy presence my light.

By Thou my Wisdom, Thou my true Word;
I ever with Thee, Thou with me, Lord;
Thou my great Father, I thy true son;
Thou in me dwelling, and I with Thee one.

Be Thou my battleshield, sword for the fight;
Be Thou my dignity, Thou my delight,
Thou my soul's shelter, Thou my high tower:
Raise Thou me heavenward, O Power of my power.

Riches I heed not, nor man's empty praise;
Thou mine inheritance, now and always:
Thou and Thou only, first in my heart,
High King of heaven, my treasure Thou art.

High King of heaven, after victory won,
May I reach heav'n's joys, O bright heaven's Sun!
Heart of my own heart, whatever befall,
Still be my Vision, O Ruler of all.

Ancient Irish hymn
tr. E. H. Hull (1860-1935)
versified by M. E. Byrne (1880-1931)

APPENDICES

Reflections on Critical Approaches to the Sermon on the Mount

Many readers of the Christian Bible pore over its pages for no other reason than to discover theological truth and to be spiritually refreshed. Well and good; if we do not read this book with such ends in view, we are mistreating it. Nevertheless, a closer reading of the New Testament prompts a host of critical questions as well. By "critical" I do not refer to negative judgments or a critical (i.e., judgmental) spirit. Rather, I use the expression "critical questions" in a technical sense, to refer to such considerations as authorship, date, destination, sources (if any), and literary relationships to other works. To ask such questions of the documents which make up the Bible is neither a necessary mark of piety, nor a necessary mark of impiety. For the most part, they are questions which arise because the material is there.

Often when I have taken a passage of Scripture like Matthew's account of the Sermon on the Mount, and expounded it to laymen, someone has come up to me after a few sessions and asked questions like these: Isn't Luke 6:20-49 Luke's account of the Sermon on the Mount? Why then does he say it took place on a plain, a level place (Luke 6:17), and not on a mountain? Why is his account much shorter than Matthew's? Why does Matthew record eight positive beatitudes (Matt. 5:3-12), whereas Luke records only four positive beatitudes and four corresponding "woes" (Luke 6:20-26)? Why isn't the wording the same in other passages, where Matthew and Luke are recording the same teaching but in slightly different vocabulary? Why does Matthew put the so-called "golden rule" toward the end of his account (7:12), while Luke puts it in the middle (Luke 6:31)? And why does Luke leave out the words, "for this sums up the Law and the Prophets"? Why doesn't Luke record the Lord's model prayer? Or rather, why, when he does record it, does he put it in an entirely different context, where it appears as Jesus' response to his disciples' request to be taught to pray (Luke 11:1ff.)? Why are many of the verses in Matthew 5–7 not found in Luke 6:20-49 at all, but are scattered throughout Luke's Gospel? If the Sermon on the Mount is so significant, why don't Mark and John record it as well? Did

Matthew read Luke's Gospel before writing his own? Or vice versa? Or neither? Just who is Matthew?

I do not intend to give detailed answers to these questions. To even begin to do so would double the length of this book. In this brief appendix I intend simply to outline some of the principles that lie behind the answers. Also, I want to sketch in some of the developments in contemporary New Testament scholarship, including some approaches and some conclusions which I judge invalid and which will not, in my opinion, stand the test of time.

I shall start by providing two charts. The first begins with the Sermon on the Mount recorded by Matthew, and shows the distribution of that material (or very similar material) in Luke's Gospel. The second begins with the Sermon as it appears in Luke's Gospel, and shows how his material is distributed in Matthew's Gospel.

CHART ONE

Matthew 5–7	Luke
5:3-12	6:20-26
5:13	14:34f.
5:14-16	8:16
5:17-20	16:16f.
5:21-26	12:57-59
5:27-32	(16:18)
5:33-37	—
5:38-42	6:29f.
5:43-48	6:27f., 32-36
6:1-4	—
6:5f.	—
6:7-15	11:1-4
6:16-18	—
6:19-21	12:33f.
6:22f.	11:34-36
6:24	16:13
6:25-34	12:22-32
7:1-5	6:37-42
7:6	—
7:7-11	11:19-13
7:12	6:31
7:13f.	13:23f.
7:15-20 (cf.12:33-35)	6:43-45
7:21-23	6:46; 13:25-27
7:24-27	6:47-49

CHART TWO

Luke 6:20-49	Matthew
6:20-23	5:3-6,11f.
6:27-30	5:39b-42
6:31	7:12
6:32-36	5:44-48
6:37f.	7:1f.
6:39f.	—
6:41f.	7:3-5
6:43-45	7:16-20
6:46	7:21
6:47-49	7:24-27

It is worthwhile pausing to pick up a copy of the New Testament and to examine each of these pairs. You will quickly discover that the charts make the problem simpler than it really it. To take one example: although I have put Luke 11:1-4 beside Matthew 6:7-15, Luke actually omits some of the material in Matthew 6:7-15. His wording in this case is a little different, even though both writers say approximately the same thing. And to top it off, his context is completely different.

For many modern writers, these problems become occasions to engender a profound skepticism. Some contemporary scholars think that Jesus actually did preach a great sermon, which was variously preserved by Matthew and Luke who used common source document(s). Many others, however, think no such sermon was ever preached. It is common to suggest that Matthew 5–7 is largely an amalgam of snippets from perhaps twenty of Jesus' sermons. In this view, Matthew's setting is a literary fiction. Another popular argument is that most of the material comes from the early church, but not from Jesus at all. This view argues that the so-called "Sermon on the Mount" is simply a collection of church catechetical material, pulled together about A.D. 90 and ascribed to Jesus partly out of popular (but mistaken) belief, and partly to give the material more authority.

A related question must be introduced, namely, the Synoptic Problem. Matthew, Mark, and Luke are the so-called "Synoptic Gospels." Close study of these three Gospels demonstrates that they are close enough to one another in wording and order of events that some sort of literary relationship exists among the three. Consensus holds (rightly, I think) that Mark was written first, and that Matthew and Luke had at least read Mark's Gospel before composing their own. In addition, Matthew and Luke have a great deal of material in common which is not found in Mark. This material, most commonly designated Q (for *Quelle*, a German word meaning "source"), is mostly made up of sayings of Jesus. It is disputed whether there was one written source which both Matthew and Luke used, or whether there were many different sources. The arguments are complex, and I have no desire to repeat them here. But it should be noted that the Sermon on the Mount is Q-material.

To talk of "sources" and "literary dependence" should not be alarming: Luke, at least, records his own dependence both on eyewitness accounts and on literary sources (Luke 1:1-4).

Contemporary New Testament scholarship goes beyond this fundamental question. It observes that different kinds of literary material tend to fall into classifiable literary forms. "Form criticism," as the study of literary forms is called, is in the first instance largely descriptive. Unfortunately, however, in the hands of many form critics, the merely descriptive becomes the prescriptive. These citics start saying that certain forms *ought* to be there. Moreover, if there are two accounts of the Lord's Model Prayer, they begin to ask which is earlier, according to the literary form each possesses. Then they take guesses at what the "original" is likely to be. And then they ask what changes Matthew and Luke performed on this original, and on this basis try to deduce how Matthew's theology differs from Luke's, and so forth.

To add to the immensity of the related problems, the force of any scholar's presuppositions needs to be taken into account. Not a few contemporary New Testament scholars have gone on record as denying the possibility of miracles, the existence of angels, the deity of Christ, and much more. They realize the New Testament affirms such things, but they protest that such beliefs are cultural relics of a pre-scientific age, and that the *real* message of Christianity in no way depends on such beliefs.

For my part, I remain convinced that such presuppositions reflect accommodation to contemporary secularism, and are in no way demanded by the evidence. The Bible's own witness to itself is that it is the Word of God; and its own evidence, not to speak of correlative evidence, I find quite overwhelming. It becomes important, then, to try to understand this book on its own terms, and to avoid as many twentieth century prejudices as possible, lest we get it to say only what we want to hear. I must here avoid the question of how to interpret this Word from God, except to say that the ordinary rules of grammar and philology, and the ordinary canons of historical criticism, may be safely applied to it in order to understand better all that it affirms.

The radical skepticism of certain critics, therefore, I find unacceptable on many grounds. However, this still leaves us with the Synoptic Problem; with the genuine insights of form criticism; with the relationship of

Matthew 5–7 to Luke 6:20-49, and with the relationship of both of them to an alleged written Q; and so forth. Although the Scripture (not just the men who wrote it) is God-breathed; and although holy men of God spoke as they were carried along by the Holy Spirit (II Tim. 3:16; II Peter 2:20); yet the divine activity was such that Paul wrote in Paul's style, to respond to the needs he saw in the churches. Matthew wrote according to his own interests. And Luke was not exempted from the tiring work of research (Luke 1:1-4).

I propose, therefore, to sketch in some observations which may make it easier for the general reader to come to terms with the disparate data, and yet retain—even reinforce—his confidence in the Word of God. My focus will zero in on the Sermon on the Mount. I must again insist that this is a light sketch. Detailed help can be sought elsewhere.

First: Most likely Jesus preached primarily, if not exclusively, in Aramaic, a dialect of Hebrew. The New Testament documents were written in Greek. As anyone who has done any translation can testify, the probability of variant readings in different translations of the same material is overwhelming. If the Q material did indeed stand in several written sources, how many of those sources were written in Aramaic? What effect would this have on the finished Gospels of Matthew and Luke? At least some variations are to be accounted for in this manner.

Second: We usually have preserved for us, not verbatim records of all that Jesus said on any particular occasion, but highly condensed reports. If we may accept that Matthew 5–7 gives us a resume of what Jesus preached on a certain hillside in Galilee, it needs to be pointed out that these chapters take only fifteen minutes to read—even if one is a slow reader. The occasion pictured in Matthew 5–7 sounds like a full-fledged teach-in. Undoubtedly it went on for hours, with Jesus preaching the equivalent of many of our sermons. I could well believe, for example, that the beatitudes were points of a larger message, or pithy conclusions to major topics. Perhaps there were other points omitted by the condensed reports we have in hand. I have no difficulty theorizing that the woes of Luke's account were embedded in this preaching. In other parts of the Sermon, if Luke leaves out more than Matthew, both leave out much more than was there.

Third: The Synoptic Problem is a desperately complex issue, honeycombed with many uncertainties and speculations. That first century writers should borrow from one another on such a wholesale scale is no problem; that was customary enough in the ancient world (compare, for example, Jude and II Peter 2). The problem is much deeper. The Synoptic Problem has never been "solved," and probably never will be—there are just too many unknowns. It does not in any way vitiate faith; but it

does make explanations about literary relationships extremely complicated.*

Related to this problem is the question of authorship. Luke's Gospel
was not written by an apostle; what of Matthew's Gospel? The Gospel itself does not claim Matthean authorship, so we cannot be sure. External
evidence supports a very early belief that the apostle Matthew did in
fact write it, and evidence thought to contradict this tradition is not as
strong as some people think.† Others date it late and ascribe it to unknown authors because this would, in their view, reduce its historical
credibility. I point these things out, not to offer easy answers to each
question, but to indicate that discussion about the relationship between
Matthew 5–7 and Luke 6:20-49 touches on some very difficult issues.
Glib answers should be avoided.

Fourth: The Evangelists themselves have their own purposes in writing. Although they are describing select parts of the life, ministry, death,
and resurrection of one man, Jesus of Nazareth, yet they frame their
work in somewhat different vocabularies. They aim at different reader-
ships, and they include material and exclude material according to their
own purposes and interests. Moreover, they sometimes arrange their nar-
ratives chronologically, and sometimes topically. As a result, a particular
miracle may get moved by one Evangelist to a different part of his story,
simply because if fits in better with the theme with which he is then concerned.

We do the same thing today, although perhaps not to the same extent.
I have just finished reading Antonia Fraser's excellent biography,
Cromwell: Our Chief of Men. Once Cromwell has become Lord Protec-
tor, she divides up her next few chapters into a topical arrangement
which examines Cromwell's rule from various perspectives. Each of these
chapters covers the entire period of that rule; they cannot be read
chronologically.

In older liberal commentaries, whenever a particular Evangelist left
something out, it was common to read such words as these: "Luke didn't
know about that," or, "This saying was not in Matthew's source." Now,
however, there is a more sensitive recognition of the fact that an Evangelist might leave out an account or omit certain details simply because it
doesn't suit his purposes to put them in. The four Evangelists provide us
with four "theologies" which complement one another and provide us
with a multiform testimony to the person and work of the Lord Jesus
Christ. We ought to be grateful that the Spirit of God has overseen their

---

*The interested reader may profitably turn to some such book as Donald Guthrie's
New Testament Introduction.
†Compare N. B. Stonehouse, *Origins of the Synoptic Gospels*.

work in such a way that we have received a series of portraits of inexhaustible richness.

Sadly enough, not a few New Testament scholars, newly aware of the theology of each Evangelist, pit theology against history. Every little difference becomes a clue to wildly speculative theological motifs, whereas the simplest harmonization may be the better route to follow. If Jesus goes *up* on a *mountainside* and *sits* in Matthew, and comes *down* to a *level place* and *stands* in Luke (Matt. 5:1; Luke 6:17) must we hypothesize all sorts of deep symbolism? Perhaps he started off doing the former, but touched by the needs of the crowd that would not let him alone (Luke 6:18f.), he did the latter, and continued his discourse. Half a dozen other possibilities come to mind. It is certain, in any case, that both Matthew and Luke give the impression that the material they present from Jesus' teaching is a fair synopsis of parts of that teaching *as uttered on that particular occasion.* It is both unnecessary and, methodologically speaking, quite improper to suppose that Matthew 5–7 is an amalgam of isolated sayings vaguely remembered by the church and melted together by Matthew and Luke to make up a sort of sample sermon which Jesus never preached. The Evangelists do not tell us this is a sample of Jesus' teaching, even though they sometimes introduce Jesus' parables with the vagueness appropriate to that idea. No, they make the Sermon on the Mount historically specific. This is typical of the fact that the Evangelists were, under God, both historians and theologians.

Fifth: Whatever else he was, Jesus of Nazareth was an itinerant preacher. This is not to deny that he was more; it is simply an emphatic way of underscoring his *modus operandi*. That means he preached the same sorts of messages again and again, in town after town and city after city. Undoubtedly the same themes came up repeatedly, and even many of the same arresting phrases.

I was involved in a part-time itinerant ministry for several years. I know firsthand how the same sermons get honed and adapted, repeated and variously applied, as the itinerant preacher moves from center to center. Entire paragraphs came out almost exactly the way they did in the last town. Changes may be accidental, or they may be premeditated.

I believe this is one of the most overlooked features of the ministry of Jesus Christ as recorded in our Gospels. (Perhaps this is because too few New Testament scholars have done much itinerant preaching!) If part of the message of Jesus in Matthew's account of the Sermon on the Mount is found in another context in Luke, it may simply mean that Jesus preached the same thing more than once. Sometimes even the discovery of an ordered pair of associated ideas in different contexts in the two Gospels indicates nothing more than that Jesus himself paired off the two ideas in that way.

Consider the Lord's model prayer. Luke definitely associates his version of that prayer with the disciples' request for instruction (Luke 11:1-4). Matthew's version of it places it in the middle of the Sermon on the Mount (Matt. 6:9-13). How are we to account for the difference?

According to what we've seen so far, several possibilities are open to us: (1) Matthew borrowed from Luke (or, less likely, vice versa), or they both borrowed from a common source. This means that the setting in at least one of these two Gospels is artificial. This view is popular enough. However, quite apart from presuppositions about the nature of Scripture, I must ask if this is the most likely solution, the solution most sensitive to the historical realities of Jesus' itinerant ministry. I would argue strongly to the contrary, especially if, as I think, these two books were written when there were still enough eyewitnesses around to set the record straight.

(2) Luke's setting is historically accurate. Matthew records a resumé of a sermon preached by Jesus in the setting he describes in chapter 5, but includes *some* other material, including the Lord's model prayer, which Jesus did not actually teach on that occasion, but which suited the context well enough. In other words, Matthew adds at least a little material into his resumé, such material being authentic in the sense that it is indeed the teaching of Jesus, but inauthentic in the sense that it did not orginally belong to this historical context. Matthew has introduced it here because of topical considerations typical of his methods. And after all, doesn't my own outline of Matthew 5–7 suggest that 6:9-15 is something of an excursus?

(3) Alternatively, Jesus taught the model prayer in this early sermon; but it was something he needed to teach again. After all, Matthew 5–7 has a good deal to say about humility, yet Jesus' disciples failed to learn much about this lesson the first time around. Jesus had to return to the theme more than once. I have no difficulty believing the disciples were equally slow in learning to pray; and, coming to Jesus for help in Luke 11, he may well have taught the same basic form as he had earlier outlined in Matthew 6.

What then shall we say of the internal differences between the Lord's Model Prayer as recorded in Matthew, and as recorded in Luke? It is interesting to observe that scholarly critics who rely heavily on form criticism are divided as to which form came first. Therefore, their criteria cannot be as objective as they would sometimes have us believe. Moreover, if (2), above, is correct, then Luke's form came first; and that possibility cannot simply be dismissed. But if (3) is correct, the question is irrelevant: there remains no reason why both cannot be authentic.

In this connection, it is worth noting that the function to which any particular saying is put helps to define its context. Sometimes the Evangelists appear to be offering detached sayings to illustrate a point; but when they nail down the time and place in which Jesus said such-and-such, I take it they expect the reader to believe their testimony is an accurate reflection of what he said, or of part of what he said, on that occasion. They are telling us that the immediate function of a particular saying, or at least part of that function, has been preserved in its historical setting. Arguments which ignore this observation are tampering with the objective evidence in favor of speculative theories.

Sixth: There is in the Gospels much more internal evidence supporting their general historical reliability than is often recognized. I deeply regret that some books demonstrating this fact have not received the wide distribution they deserve. And even where there is minor difference and no direct literary dependence between two Gospel accounts, we have testimony of increased strength, not contradiction; for the absence of collusion in such instances means there is multiple attestation.

Another factor deserves weighing. In teaching Africans and Asians in a Western setting, I have observed that they excel wherever rote learning is required. But they are not as strong when it comes to understanding and formulating abstract concepts. Of course, I am generalizing; but I have talked over the problem with Asian and African nationals doing graduate work in our seminary, and they acknowledge the basic difference in educational approach. The difference is not genetic; second and third generation Asians do not seem to enjoy any special ability to memorize, nor to labor under any conceptual handicap. (Investigation of these phenomena in depth would be worth pursuing.)

In first-century Palestine, education was heavily oriented toward rote learning. Some have even tried to argue that Jesus trained his disciples to memorize all his teachings in the same way that Jewish rabbis memorized the entire Hebrew Bible (the Old Testament) plus great masses of traditional material. Although this theory goes too far, there can be little doubt that Jesus' disciples were indeed capable of memorizing vast amounts of material quickly, even when they did not understand it all right away. I believe this observation helps sustain the historical credibility of the eyewitnesses on whom Luke, for example, relied. Moreover, the fixity of the oral forms which characterized some of the gospel material before it was reduced to writing is better understood in terms of such an ability to memorize, than in terms of stylized "forms" which would often take many more decades to develop than the evidence will allow.

Finally: The positions held by most scholars, of whatever persuasion, are the result of a tight interlocking of various bits and pieces of hard evidence, deductions, speculations, and presuppositions. Even the wildest bit of theorizing can begin to appear credible if it can be made to cohere with a larger structure.

Because of these interlocking chains, to overturn someone else's theory is a major undertaking. We all need to admit that we are capable of being quite mistaken, and even self-deceived, in our own chains of argument. Such an admission will evoke attention to detail and a return to the hard evidence; and perhaps it will also mitigate arrogance.

Having observed that dangers are built into these interlocking structures, we also derive some benefit from them; for careful work will often reveal how some opposing position, at first sight impregnable, is in reality a tight chain made up of a few solid facts and a large number of highly doubtful links.

For example, one very competent scholar pictures the church putting together the teachings of the Sermon on the Mount in present codified form, largely in reaction to the Council of Jamnia, about A.D. 90, even though Jesus' death, resurrection and ascension took place before A.D. 30. This Council of Jamnia is alleged to be a turning point in Jewish history, when opposition to Christianity hardened and the decisions were made regarding what books would be admitted to the Hebrew canon. However, although two councils did convene in Jamnia, it is in my judgment very doubtful if either had much to do with the Old Testament canon (except to air difficulties); and equally, Jamnia merely reflected a long-since established opposition to Christianity. A growing body of evidence now supports these contentions, calling into question the earlier assumptions. We might also ask, why was the church so long (some sixty years!) in formulating its relationship to Old Testament prophecies? What evidence is there that Jesus himself did *not* teach such things as those found in Matthew 5–7?

For a second example, let us follow what another distinguished scholar makes of Matthew 7:7-11 (Luke 11:9-13), concerning asking, seeking knocking, and the Father's eagerness to give good gifts. He thinks that the Q-material of Matthew and Luke was actually found in one document, Q. He notes that in Luke, this particular passage, Luke 11:9-13, is found in a section on prayer (Luke 11:1-13) following the Lord's Model Prayer (Luke 11:2-4) and the parable of the friend at midnight (Luke 11:5-8). Why, then, does this passage appear where it does in Matthew (7:7-11), quite separated from the model prayer (6:9-13), but following hard after a saying about not giving holy things to dogs (7:6), and just before the "Golden Rule" (7:12)? He acknowledges that no completely satisfactory answer can be given, but offers a conjecture. He thinks the natural place for Matthew 7:7-11 would be right after the Lord's Model Prayer (6:9-13). However, because Matthew puts something else after that prayer, the warning about an unforgiving spirit

(6:14f.)—which, admittedly, equally suits that context—Matthew is left with the material of 7:7-11 on his hands and no place to put it. Matthew finally decides to put it in an unsuitable context—where it is now.

At first sight this seems plausible enough; but a few questions weaken the conjecture considerably. If Matthew had this material in hand, and if the obvious place for it was right after the model prayer, why didn't he at least put it after 6:14f., the saying on forgiveness? Wouldn't the context still have been prayer? Is the present context (7:7-11) so very unsuitable? I have tried to show in my exposition that the flow of thought in Matthew 5–7 is remarkably coherent, despite the fact it is only a resumé of a much more extended discourse. And besides, I remain unconvinced that the Q-material came from one document anyway. I confess I remain persuaded that Jesus gave this material in the context of his most famous sermon, and, quite likely, in the context of Luke 11 as well.

✿　　✿　　✿

In his famous poem, *The Everlasting Mercy*, John Masefield included these lines:

> For while the Plough tips round the Pole
> The trained mind outs the upright soul,
> As Jesus said the trained mind might,
> Being wiser than the sons of light.
> But trained men's minds are stretched so thin
> They let all sorts of darkness in;
> Whatever light man finds they doubt it,
> They love not light, but talk about it.

This sweeping judgment goes too far: I have met both untrained men and trained men with "upright souls." Behind Masefield's lines, however, there lurks a real danger. That danger is the temptation to make human reason autonomous.

Lest I be accused of pleading for the irrational, I hasten to add that we human beings are responsible to use our reason to the best of our abilities. But if the Bible's presentation of God be true, then no man, and no man's reason, has the right to be autonomous—there is not even the possibility of being genuinely autonomous. In fact, every effort to become so is part and parcel of our rebellion.

This is not the place to defend such a perspective. I simply wish to emphasize that the more years I put into the study of the Scripture, the more I find myself under its authority and judged by it, rather than the authority over it with competence to judge it.

Reflections on Theological Interpretations of the Sermon on the Mount

Over the years the Sermon on the Mount has been interpreted in a remarkable number of ways. A rapid sketch of the most significant of these theological interpretations may help to explain why I have proceeded as I have.

Some have argued that the Sermon on the Mount is an "interim ethic." That is, Jesus advocated the radical ethics of these chapters because he expected the consummated eschatological age to begin imminently. This ethical stance was to be adopted by his followers in the very short period that remained before the arrival of the end. The terrible urgency of this expectation demanded utter commitment and superhuman righteousness for this climactic period. However, Jesus was mistaken; the end did not arrive. By the same token, the unyielding demands of this "interim ethic" must be dismissed as quite impossible for people today, whose ordinary conduct is not controlled by this expectation of the end. Literal fulfillment of the Sermon on the Mount is absurd if the world actually continues to plod on for more than a few weeks or months.

This view is not as popular as it once was. Many people have noted its weaknesses. The Sermon on the Mount nowhere limits its ethic to an interim period. More important, Jesus was not a fanatical enthusiast whose moral values were totally determined by his expectation of imminent catastrophe; the tension between the "already" aspects of the kingdom and the "not yet" aspects run right back to Jesus himself. Therefore he expected a community to be formed, a community which lived under the authority of the already in-breaking kingdom, in expectation of the consummation of that kingdom. In fact, the substance of Jesus' ethic is designed not only for the period until his second advent, but for all eternity; for although heaven and earth may pass away, Jesus' words will never pass away.

A second interpretation of the Sermon on the Mount is the existential interpretation. According to this view, the Sermon is not to be taken as an authoritative exposition of concrete ethical principles, but a challenge to personal decision. It orients life to an "eschatological" perspective; but by "eschatological" the theological existentialists do not mean that the age to come must be taken seriously, or that it has already overlapped the present age. In fact, these temporal categories of eschatology are utterly rejected as mythical constructions. Eschatology is reinterpreted; the biblical tension between the present life and the end-time judgment is displaced by a tension between the life and conduct that now is and the life and conduct that ought to be. But what "ought to be" is not formulated in terms of the propositions of the Sermon on the Mount, but in terms of an attitude of openness to the future that brings with it constant self-examination and repentance.

I confess I find it very difficult to be sympathetic to this approach. If theological existentialism wishes to construct its own ethical models, well and good; but it should avoid foisting its models onto the New Testament. According to this view, propositional revelation is in principle impossible—as is the supernatural intervention of a personal/infinite God. Accordingly, the bibical data are filtered through a grid designed to remove all such material and launder it ("demythologize it"). The resulting structure accords nicely with modern existential categories, but very poorly with the biblical texts themselves.

A third approach insists that the Sermon on the Mount is meant for this entire age, and that it is to be rigorously obeyed. Most frequently the adherents to this view divide into two groups. The one argues that the Sermon on the Mount is law and not gospel, and as such is not really compatible with Pauline theology. Jesus and Paul, according to this view, cannot walk together. In fact, Paul is guilty of distorting Jesus' teaching. The other group is often associated with the Anabaptist tradition. It takes the Sermon on the Mount to be an accurate reflection of the divine will, to be obeyed both privately and corporately. It holds that salvation is by grace through faith, but that the necessary manifestation of this salvation is a life lived in conformity to the precepts of the Sermon on the Mount. Usually pacifism constitutes part of this stance; and therefore, if God has given the sword to the state (Rom. 13:1ff.), it follows that Christians must not only refrain from participation in military and police forces, but must equally avoid all civic positions which would require decisions in any way associated with such forces.

Both of these perspectives take the Sermon on the Mount seriously. I find myself differing from the first, however, because it does not take salvation history sufficiently seriously. To allege antagonism between the teaching of Jesus and the teaching of Paul is to be insensitive to the progress of revelation brought about by Christ's cross-work, resurrection, and ascension. Such a view ignores the eschatological dimensions of Jesus' own preaching, and the heavy stress in the Sermon on the Mount itself on poverty of spirit, the importance of asking and seeking. It ignores the Sermon's recognition of the need for grace.

The second perspective, the Anabaptist/Mennonite tradition, I find very attractive. Nevertheless, my own exposition of the Sermon on the Mount has shown where I must part company with it. I think its view is insensitive to the antithetical manner in which Jesus often preaches, and therefore reads more into the text than what either Jesus or Matthew would defend. The Sermon by itself is not a final comment on such issues as war and capital punishment—there are other bibical considerations. Moreover, to make the prohibition of such things an essential part of moral law seems to argue either for moral development in God, or for a development in what God commands. This is of fundamental importance, for it suggests that earlier commands by God were actually in contradiction to his real will. If morality is not directly related to what God really approves, but only to what he commands, a terrible tension is set up in ✓ him. Moreover, the New Testament treatment of the church does not require that Christian people be quite as removed from, say, politics, as this perspective seems to suggest.

A fourth answer to the meaning of the Sermon on the Mount is that advanced by Lutheran orthodoxy. This claims that the Sermon is an impossibly high ideal designed to make men aware of their sin and turn to Christ for forgiveness. The sermon, then, is essentially a preparation for the gospel. This view does justice to some of the relationships between Jesus and Paul; but it sounds more like the conclusion of systematic theology applied a trifle too soon, than the exegesis of the text.

A fifth approach is that of classic liberalism, popular at the turn of the century. Orthodoxy, which placed emphasis on man's need for redemption, the atoning death of Christ, and a supernatural new birth, was displaced by an optimistic liberalism which saw the Sermon on the Mount as the real gospel, the gospel in a nutshell. The Sermon was thought to be the essential map for building a progressive civilization. But this dream of classic liberalism was shattered by two world wars. Liberalism overlooked the fact that human nature requires forgiveness *and help.* Fed by an optimistic faith in the inevitability of evolutionary development, liberalism actually displaced the real gospel with a secular philosophy of progress. Quite unaware of the subjectivity of its choices, it selected those parts of the biblical revelation conducive to its spirit and theory, and rejected the rest. The result provided man with no Savior, no Redeemer, no divine grace, no empowering Spirit; but only a lovely pattern which men subsequently learned they were not able to copy on their own strength.

A more recent view interprets the Sermon on the Mount as catechetical material prepared by the church, some of which stretches back to the historical Jesus. Because the Sermon was catechetical material, according to this view, it was in every case preceded by the proclamation of the gospel and by personal conversion. The gospel precedes the ethical demands of the Sermon on the Mount. Jesus' call to discipleship is therefore directed only at those for whom the power of Satan has already been destroyed by the gospel and who are already heirs of the kingdom of God.

The chief problem with this interpretation is that it does not treat the Gospel of Matthew as a serious historical (as well as theological) document. If Jesus never did preach a Sermon on the Mount, nor even provide the essential content embedded in Matthew 5–7, then it may be legitimate to hypothesize that the Pauline emphasis on grace, salvation, conversion, and transformation precedes the "catechetical" material of the Sermon on the Mount. But if he did, then even if his material has been somewhat framed by the church's concern for the catechizing of new converts, it is illegitimate to explain away the theological relevance of Jesus' preaching in its first historical setting by appealing to such catechesis.

By now it will be fairly clear where my own exposition has agreed with the above interpretations and where it differs, even if the foregoing survey has been painfully brief. I accept the Lutheran position as a partial explanation: the Sermon on the Mount does indeed drive men and women to a sober recognition of their sin and a realistic understanding of their need for grace. But the Sermon does more than that. It portrays the pattern of conduct under kingdom authority, a pattern that demands conformity *now*, even if perfection will not be achieved until the kingdom's consummation. In that sense I agree with the Anabaptist tradition. In my judgment, however, that tradition runs into serious difficulty in its attempt at formulating the relationship between law in the Old Testament and law in the New. As I indicated in the second chapter, I take it that Jesus sees himself and his teaching as that toward which the Old Testament Scriptures point.

Moreover, I think that the norms of the kingdom, worked out in the lives of the heirs of the kingdom to constitute the witness of the kingdom, touches society a little more trenchantly than the Anabaptist tradition allows. If my view overlaps anywhere with the interpretation of the sermon advanced by classic liberalism, it is in this area—even if I can endorse neither liberalism's naive optimism nor its rejection of supernatural salvation. That men must respond to the probing of the Sermon on the Mount is much stressed by the existentialist approach; and with that stress I concur, although I must divorce myself utterly from the unsubstantiality of the probe as construed by theological existentialism. The urgency of obedience perceived by the proponents of the "interim ethic" structure is undeniably important; but the urgency depends, not on the false model of eschatology advanced by this position, but on the prospect of coming judgment whose timing is unknown but whose decision and sentence are irrevocable.

There is one more theological interpretation of the Sermon on the ⑦ Mount that needs to be mentioned, if only because it is so popular, especially in North America. It is the view of dispensationalism. This view rigidly distinguishes the period of law (Sinai to Calvary) from the period of grace (Calvary to the second advent). When Jesus came proclaiming the kingdom of heaven, he was in fact offering a millennial kingdom to Jews. The Sermon on the Mount is seen as the law which pertains to that millennial kingdom. However, because the Jews as a whole did not accept Jesus as their King and Messiah, Jesus went into a second plan, hitherto utterly unforeseen by Old Testament revelation and known only to the secret counsels of God. In pursuit of this secret plan, Jesus delayed the coming of the millennial kingdom and introduced an age of grace, the "kingdom in a mystery." This kingdom may be designated the kingdom of God, not the kingdom of heaven. As a result of this theological structure, the Sermon on the Mount has no *immediate* revelance or application to the Christian. It is usually conceded that the Sermon embraces principles of conduct which do apply to us; but its real intent is to serve as law during the coming millennial reign. Of the various entailments of this theological structure, one is the conclusion that Matthew 6:14f. must be taken as a formal legal stipulation which governs the conditions under which forgiveness may be granted. As such, these verses are antithetical to the age of grace.

Dispensationalism is a powerful movement today. It enjoys many godly exponents, and some scholarly ones. It is characterized by a desire to treat the Scriptures seriously, a laudable attitude. However, although it no doubt affords valuable insights, I find myself quite definitely opposed to its overall structure. As this is not the place to enter into prolonged debate, I shall simply offer a short selection of reasons why I cannot accept the dispensational interpretation of the Sermon on the Mount.

First: The dispensational interpretation of the Sermon on the Mount depends so heavily on the structure of accepted dispensationalism that it is insensitive to the text itself. In other words, the movement imposes its theological construction onto the biblical data, in a manner quite reminiscent of far less conservative groups. This, I submit, is true of its interpretation of the entire Bible, but it is more particularly true in its approach to Matthew's Gospel. Moreover, this theological construction is so all-embracing that it is extremely difficult for a member of this school of thought to accept a different interpretation of any particular passage without endangering the entire system. As a result, a certain rigidity is frequently observed, the total dispensational package becoming equivalent to orthodoxy itself as far as many of its proponents are concerned.

In dispensationalism, the interpretation of Matthew's Gospel is one of the crucial support pillars of the theological structure. Remove it (or any one of a dozen other pillars), and the structure collapses. Dispensational theologians say that up to Matthew 12, Jesus offers the millennial kingdom (= the kingdom of heaven) to the Jews. Unfortunately, however, they reject him; and so toward the end of Matthew 12, he rejects them. In Matthew 13 Jesus is found unfolding the "secrets of the kingdom," i.e., the kingdom hitherto hidden from view, but more or less equivalent to the kingdom that I have expounded.

More recent dispensational writers admit that "kingdom of heaven" and "kingdom of God" are frequently interchangeable, but still insist that there is enough difference between them to sustain the view that the former refers to the millennial kingdom and the latter to the hidden, saving reign. This I cannot accept. "Kingdom of heaven" is Matthew's preferred use, "kingdom of God" the preference of other New Testament writers (cf. Matt. 4:17; 10:6f.; Mark 1:15; Luke 9:2). Not only are the two expressions found in synoptic parallels, but there is a broader *historical* consideration. Why is the millennial kingdom = kingdom of heaven concept offered during the early part of Jesus' ministry in only Matthew's Gospel? If, for example, any harmonization between John and Matthew is possible, then John 3 must precede Matthew 5–7; yet John 3 is already talking about the kingdom of God in such categories of salvation as new birth, belief, and the Spirit.

Moreover, to argue that the Sermon on the Mount is law in the sense that it is a legal prescription for the millennium is to confuse certain basic issues. To pit law, righteousness, and peace as kingdom concepts against grace and belief as salvation concepts is to create an antithesis that the New Testament writers will not tolerate. According to Paul, for example, salvation has always been by grace, even when God's people were under the Mosaic legislation. And salvation, however construed, has always demanded the conformity to the will of God portrayed in Matthew 5–7. Hence, to take, say, Matthew 6:14f. as evidence of legal prescription *as opposed to grace* is, biblically speaking, unjustifiable.

Second: A close study of the Sermon on the Mount suggests that Jesus has in view just such a world as our own as the sphere in which to work out his demands. The Sermon presupposes a world in which there is persecution of all followers of Jesus without exception, gross insults, anger, personal litigation, adultery, lying, vengeful attitudes, malice, religious hypocrisy, insincere prayers, love of money, worry, judgmentalism, false prophets, and much more. As Carl F. H. Henry puts it, "An era requiring special principles to govern face-slapping and turning the other cheek

(5:39) is hardly one to which the term 'millenium' is aptly applied." Matthew 5–7 envisions *our* world, not a reign of millennial splendor.

Third: A close study of the Sermon on the Mount gives the impression that Jesus Christ is repeatedly emphasizing the lasting validity of his words, rather than indicating that their main concerns may well have to be postponed. The Sermon overflows with present imperatives, with the refrain "But I say unto you," indicating the importance of continued obedience.

Finally: I judge dispensationalism to be particularly insensitive to the ways in which the New Testament uses the Old. This subject is so vast I hesitate even to raise it. Nevertheless I am persuaded that the New Testament writers, whether Matthew or Paul, uniformly see the church as the sole legitimate successor to believing Israel, the people of God in the Old Testament. In so doing they cite many Old Testament passages which they claim *are being fulfilled in Christ's atoning work, resurrection, and the resulting church.* Matthew 5:17-20 fits into this pattern quite easily; it does not fit easily into any other pattern.

None of these points is offered as an argument which demolishes dispensational theology once and for all. I am well aware of the responses which my dispensational friends and colleagues would advance—and of my counter-arguments, and so forth. But I would like to think that these few paragraphs will challenge some exponents from each position, including my own, to study the texts again, and try to listen to them from a perspective other than his customary one, the goal being to free oneself from the shackles (but not the advice) of well-worn tradition and to learn afresh from the Word of God.